LAW
&
GOVERNMENT

An Introductory Study Course

VISION FORUM
Ministries®

Second Printing
Copyright © 2011-2012 Vision Forum Ministries
All Rights Reserved

"Where there is no vision, the people perish."

The Vision Forum, Inc.
4719 Blanco Rd., San Antonio, Texas 78212
1-800-440-0022
www.visionforum.com

ISBN 978-1-937460-08-2

Cover Design and Typography by Justin Turley

Printed in the United States of America

Other Curriculum Sets from Vision Forum

WWII: D-Day and the Providence of God

The Young Ladies' Study Course for Proper Writing

Biblical Economics: A Complete Study Course by R.C. Sproul, Jr.

The History of Christianity and Western Civilization

The History of the World Collection

Into the Amazon: One Lost World, Thirty Men, Seven Mysteries

Table of Contents

Introduction

This curriculum is an extension of the Witherspoon School of Law and Public Policy, which has as its mission the training of the next generation of leaders in biblical and historical principles of Law, Ethics, and Public Policy. The Witherspoon School has had the privilege over the years to train many individuals who have gone on to be leaders in their homes, their churches, and civil government.

The course on law, ethics, and public policy is intended to train older children on how to be productive Christian statesmen in their adult life. Most young people will not take an active interest in entering the legal profession or pursuing a career as a public servant, yet each of them will play a role as citizens and statesmen in the private sector. The aim of this course is to train them to think biblically as private citizens about issues of law, ethics, and public policy and to equip them with the tools they will need to be effective in their churches and local communities. This aim to train Christians to carry out their public duty in their local communities makes this course one of a kind and is the perfect supplement to any course on History, Law, Economics, Political Science, or Theology.

This course of study includes questions and writing assignments that will help the learner engage at a deeper level the topics being presented. Selections from important historical documents have been included to foster a greater love and appreciation for the rich heritage that they will someday continue. It is my great hope that this course will communicate the importance of the topics presented in a manner that will provoke a deeper study of the issues that will extend beyond these ten lessons. For this reason this course includes a list of books and other materials at the end of each lesson that will help provide some guidance to young people as they continue a diligent study of these areas on their own.

This study is divided into seven units. Each unit will cover a different area of law, ethics and public policy.

Unit one is an introductory unit. It will cover foundational concepts of law, ethics, and public policy, which are foundational for a biblical understanding of the subject matter. This unit will cover important concepts such as the sovereign authority of God and the sufficiency of Scripture.

Unit two introduces the doctrine of jurisdictional authority. It will explain the nature and source of all authority and will explain why authority by its very nature is limited. Separate lessons are dedicated to explaining the nature of each jurisdiction of delegated authority, Family, Church, and State.

Unit three is dedicated to specific areas in which every private citizen has the ability to play a significant role. In this section students will learn the proper nature of the United States Constitution and how it is to be interpreted. It will also approach the issues of social ethics, civil resistance to tyranny, and biblical economics.

Unit four is dedicated to key concepts in the electoral system. Here students will learn the biblical framework for casting their votes. Moreover, they will learn about important aspects of the constitutional electoral process. Also in this section, students will learn about the legitimate role of women in the political process.

Unit five is dedicated to the Executive Branch of the United States Government. Students will learn the constitutional functions of the Executive Office as well as how modern presidents have exceeded the limitations placed on the office in the United States constitution.

Unit six is dedicated to the Judicial Branch of Government. In this unit, students will learn about the constitutional function of the Supreme Court. The course will also cover important issues such as the selection of judges, judicial review, and the importance of judicial precedent.

Unit seven is dedicated to the Legislative Branch. Students will be introduced to the proper constitutional powers of Congress as well as foundational concepts of law. In this unit students will learn the history of the Common Law and how it laid the foundations for American law. Finally this unit will cover the history and principles that undergirds foreign policy.

Above all else, it is my strong desire that this course will do more than teach concepts of civil government and public policy, it is my desire that students will be strengthened in their Christian faith and that through this course of study they will draw nearer to Jesus Christ. This course is not designed nor intended to train Christians to be better citizens in carrying out their civil duty to the United Sates; rather it is intended to train citizens to be better Christians in carrying out their duty to serve and glorify God in the public square. May the God of peace grant wisdom, understanding, and strength to those who undertake this course of study, and equip them to carry out His purpose in every area of their lives.

Master Outline

1. Foundations of American Government

A. Introduction to the Christian Foundations of Western Law, Part 1 —Douglas Phillips

1. Summary: A Theological and Historical Foundation

2. Outline

3. Questions

4. Selected Reading: Ben Franklin's *Appeal to the Federal Convention*

5. Definitions: Epistemology, Jurisprudence, Higher Criticism, Lower Criticism

6. Writing Assignment: Shelly Ruins in the Desert

7. Suggestions for Further Study

B. Introduction to the Christian Foundations of Western Law, Part 2 —Douglas Phillips

1. Summary: Biblical Worldview and Christian Statesman
2. Outline
3. Questions
4. Selected Reading: George Washington's *Farewell Address*
5. Definitions: Antithesis, Presupposition, Transcendence, Fideism, Epistemology
6. Writing Assignment: Persecution in the Early Church
7. Suggestions for Further Study

C. Genesis & Geneva: The Emergence of Liberty in the West —Douglas Phillips

1. Summary: Creation, Sovereignty, and Providence
2. Outline
3. Questions
4. Selected Reading: John Witherspoon's *Dominion of Providence Over the Passions of Men*
5. Definitions: Providence, Restitution, Capital Punishment
6. Writing Assignment: God's Sovereignty or Man's
7. Suggestions for Further Study

D. Symposium on the Reformation and Law —Douglas Phillips & William Einwechter

1. Summary: The Supremacy of Scripture
2. Outline
3. Questions
4. Selected Reading: *The Mayflower Compact*
5. Definitions: Commonwealth, Just War Theory
6. Writing Assignment: Christian Culture
7. Suggestions for Further Study

2. A Biblical Approach to Jurisdiction

A. Covenantal Approach to Jurisdiction

1. Summary: The Biblical Doctrine of Jurisdiction
2. Outline
3. Questions
4. Selected Reading: Samuel Adams' *The Divine Source of Liberty*
5. Definitions: Sanhedrin, Monolith, Jurisdiction
6. Written Assignment: Jurisdiction and Restraints on Civil Power
7. Suggestions For Further Study

B. An Introduction to the Theology of Church and State —Douglas Phillips

1. Summary: A Separation of Church and State
2. Outline
3. Questions
4. Selected Reading: George Gillespie's *Aaron's Rod Blossoming*
5. Definitions: Erastianism, Church Autonomy, Papal Revolution
6. Writing Assignment: Religious Liberty in Virginia
7. Suggestions for Further Study

C. The State of Parental Rights in Light of the Texas Polygamy Case —Don Hart

1. Summary: The Family
2. Outline
3. Questions
4. Selected Reading: B.M. Palmer's *The Family*
5. Definitions: Exclusionary Rule
6. Written Assignment: The Family and Civilization
7. Suggestions for Further Study

3. Christian Ethics and Public Policy

A. Biblical Law, Ethics, and Public Policy —Douglas Phillips

1. Summary: Christian Morality and the Constitution
2. Outline
3. Questions
4. Selected Reading: Cotton Mather's *Bonifacius*
5. Definitions: Ethics, Apologetics, Rationalism, Pragmatism, Gnosticism
6. Written Assignment: America is Made for a Moral People
7. Suggestions for Further Study

B. Biblical Law, Ethics, and Public Policy Recap. —Douglas Phillips

1. Summary: Biblical Faith and Social Ethics
2. Outline
3. Questions
4. Selected Reading: Augustine's *City of God*
5. Definitions: Exegesis, Hermeneutics, Bioethics
6. Written Assignment: The Bible and Science
7. Suggestions for Further Study

C. The Biblical and Historical Significance of the Second Amendment

1. Summary: Resistance to Tyranny Obedience to God
2. Outline
3. Questions
4. Selected Reading: *Magna Charta*
5. Definitions: Militia, Resistance, Tyranny
6. Written Assignment: Remembering Heroes of the Past
7. Suggestions for Further Study

D. Primer on Constitutional Money: God Over Economics

1. Summary: Biblical Economics
2. Outline
3. Questions
4. Selected Reading: Andrew Jackson's *Bank Veto Address*
5. Definitions: Fiat Money, Legal Tender, Fractional Reserve Banking.
6. Written Assignment: Special Interests
7. Suggestions for Further Study

4. Biblical Principles of Representative Government

A. The Significance of the Electoral College

1. Summary: Safeguards Against Democracy
2. Outline
3. Questions
4. Selected Reading: Oaths of English Kings
5. Definitions: Democracy, Republic, Electoral College
6. Written Assignment: Federalism
7. Suggestions for Further Study

B. What the Bible Says About Female Magistrates

1. Summary: Women's Roles in Politics
2. Outline
3. Questions
4. Selected Reading: *Monstrous Regiment of Women*
5. Definitions: Feminism, Egalitarianism
6. Written Assignment: *Bradwell v. Illinois*
7. Suggestions for Further Study

5. The Executive Office

A. A Constitutional Presidency

1. Summary: The Executive Branch
2. Outline
3. Questions
4. Selected Reading: Alexander Hamilton's *Federalist #69*
5. Definitions: Incrementalism, Impoundment
6. Written Assignment: The Religious Nature of Law
7. Suggestions for Further Study

6. Christian Jurisprudence and the Courts

A. Christian Jurisprudence: Biblical Law, Natural Law, or Positive Law?

1. Summary: The Judicial Branch
2. Outline
3. Questions
4. Selected Reading: George Gillespie's *Aaron's Rod Blossoming*
5. Definitions: Positivism, Metaphysics, Syncretism, Deism, Law
6. Written Assignment: *Griswold v. Connecticut*
7. Suggestions for Further Study

B. Christianity and the Courts?

1. Summary: The French Revolution
2. Outline
3. Questions
4. Selected Reading: Henry de Bracton's *On the Laws and Customs of England*
5. Definitions: Stare decisis, Judicial Review
6. Written Assignment: R.L. Dabney, *Ethics of the Legal Profession*
7. Suggestions for Further Study

C. Ecclesiastical Courts And Christian Arbitration

1. Summary: Church Discipline and Ecclesiastical Courts

2. Outline

3. Questions

4. Selected Reading: Patrick Henry's *Give Me Liberty or Give Me Death* Speech

5. Definitions: Canon Law, Ecclesiastical Court, Excommunication

6. Written Assignment: Church Discipline

7. Suggestions for Further Study

7. Biblical Law, Legislatures, and the Western Legal Tradition

A. The Continuing Relevance of the Law of God

1. Summary: The Legislative Branch

2. Outline

3. Questions

4. Selected Reading: Sir William Blackstone, in his *Commentaries on the Laws of England*

5. Definitions: Theonomy, General Revelation, Special Revelation

6. Written Assignment: Hammurabi Code

7. Suggestions for Further Study

B. Christianity and the Common Law

1. Summary: The Christian Foundation of the Common Law

2. Outline

3. Questions

4. Selected Reading: Westminster Confession

5. Definitions: Presupposition, Perspicuity, The Subscription Clause

6. Written Assignment: Purifying Effect of the Church on the State

7. Suggestions for Further Study

C. Biblical and Historical Background for the Law of Nations

1. Summary: God the Ruler of Nations

2. Outline

3. Questions

4. Selected Reading: *Declaration of Arbroath,* 1320

5. Definitions: Law of Nations, Sanction

6. Written Assignment: Justinian and the Concept of Sanctuary

7. Suggestions for Further Study

D. The Law of Nations and the Constitution

1. Summary: The Universal Application of God's Law

2. Outline

3. Questions

4. Selected Reading: The Monroe Doctrine

5. Definitions: Law of Beneficence and the Monroe Doctrine

6. Written Assignment: the Repentance of Manasseh

7. Suggestions for Further Study

E. The Law of Nations and American History

1. Summary: The Attributes of the Ruler of Nations

2. Outline

3. Questions

4. Selected Reading: John Calvin's *Institutes of the Christian Religion*

5. Definitions: Intermeddling, Interventionism

6. Written Assignment: Theologian Statesmen

7. Suggestions for Further Study

Booklist

Unit One

Lesson 1

For You They Signed, by Marilyn Boyer

American History to 1865, by R.J. Rushdoony

Political Sermons of the American Founding Era 1730-1805 (2 Vols.), Editor Ellis Sandoz

Christianity and the American Commonwealth: The Influence of Christianity in Making This Nation, by Charles B. Galloway

Christianity in the United States, by Daniel Dorchester

Christian Life & Character of the Civil Institutions of the United States, by Benjamin F. Morris

Lesson 2

Foundations of Christian Scholarship, Editor Gary North

Always Ready, by Greg Bahnsen

The Sufficiency of Scripture, by Joseph Stephen

Knowing Scripture, R.C. Sproul

Myths, Lies, and Half Truths, by Gary DeMar

Defending the Christian Worldview Against All Opposition, Series 1 & 2, by Greg Bahnsen

A Refutation of Pluralism, by John Brown of Haddington

Lesson 3

The Genevan Reformation and the American Founding, by David W. Hall

God, Man, and Law: the Biblical Principles, by Herbert W. Titus

Lex Rex, by Samuel Rutherford

Sovereignty, by R.J. Rushdoony

Lesson 4

Thinking Straight in a Crooked World, by Gary DeMar

The Shape of Sola Scriptura, by Keith Matheson

The Canon of Scripture, by F.F. Bruce

The Calvinistic Concept of Culture, by Henry Van Til

Sola Scriptura: The Protestant Position on the Bible, Editor, Joel R. Beeke

Unit Two

Lesson 1

This Independent Republic, by R.J. Rushdoony

Messiah the Prince, by William Symington

God and Government, by Gary DeMar

By What Standard, by Greg Bahnsen

Lesson 2

Aaron's Rod Blossoming, by George Gillespie

Letters of Samuel Rutherford, by Samuel Rutherford

The Gospel Ministry, by Thomas Foxcroft

Law and Revolution, by Harold Berman

Christ's Churches Purely Reformed, by Phillip Benedict

Lesson 3

The Family, by B. M. Palmer

The Family and Civilization, by Carl Zimmerman

From Cottage to Workstation, by Alan C. Carlson

The Puritan Family, by Edmund S. Morgan

Family Reformation, Scott Brown

Unit Three

Lesson 1

Institute on the Constitution, by John Eidsmoe

Liberty, Order, and Justice, by James McClellan

The General Principles of Constitutional Law, by Thomas Cooley

Commentaries on the United States Constitution, by Joseph Story

The Roots of Liberty, Editor, Ellis Sandoz

Lesson 2

The Divine Challenge, by John Byl

The Biblical Basis for Modern Science, by John Morris

The City of God, by Aurelius Augustine

Calvinism in History, by Nathaniel McFetridge

Ultimate Questions, by John Blanchard

Lesson 3

The Second Amendment, by David Barton

Vindiciae Contra Tyrannos, by Stephanus Janus Brutus

The Founders' Second Amendment, by Stephen Halbrook

Confrontational Politics, by Sen. H.L. Richardson, Ret

Lesson 4

Pieces of Eight, by Edwin Vieira

The Constitution of the United States with Index, by U.S. Government

The Mystery of Banking, by Murray Rothbard

Larceny of the Heart, by R.J. Rushdoony

Introduction to Christian Economics, by Gary North

Unit Four

Lesson 1

The Importance of the Electoral College, by George Grant

The Establishment and Limits of Civil Government, by James Wilson

The Roots of the American Republic, by E.C. Wines

Lesson 2

The Monstrous Regiment of Women, by John Knox

Killer Angel, by George Grant

Passionate Housewives, Desperate for God, by Jenny Chancy and Stacy McDonald

Unit Five

Lesson 1

Lives of the Presidents of the United States, by John Abbot

George Washington's Sacred Fire, by Peter A. Lillback

Life of Andrew Jackson, by John Jenkins

The Founder Constitution, Editor, Philip B. Kurland and Ralph Lerner

Unit Six

Lesson 1

The Institutes of Biblical Law, by R.J. Rushdoony

Law and Liberty, by R.J. Rushdoony

The Works of John Adams, by John Adams

Lesson 2

So Help Me God, by Chief Justice Roy Moore

Government by Judiciary, by Raoul Berger

How to Dethrone the Imperial Judiciary, by Edwin Vieira

Blackstone Commentaries on the Common Law of England, by Sir William Blackstone

Lesson 3

The Apostolic Chruch, Which Is It?, by Thomas Witherow

The Handbook of Church Discipline, by Jay A. Adams

The Church of Christ, by James Bannerman

Unit Seven

Lesson 1

The Institutes of Biblical Law, by R.J. Rushdoony

Commentaries on the Laws of England, by William Blackstone

Pierre Viret: A Forgotten Giant of the Reformation, by Jean-Marc Berthoud

Institutes of the Christian Religion, by John Calvin

Theonomy in Christian Ethics, by Greg Bahnsen

Lesson 2

Plymouth Plantation, by William Bradford

American Political Writings During the Founding Era, by Charles S. Hyneman

The American Republic: Primary Sources, by Bruce Frohnen

The Constitutional Documents of the Puritan Revolution, 1625-1660, by Samuel Rawson Gardiner

Lesson 3

Liberty and Property, by Dan Ford

Calvin on God and Political Duty, Editor, John T. McNeill

The Emergence of Liberty, by Douglas Kelly

A Common Law, by Rueben Alvarado

Lesson 4

John Calvin His Roots and Fruits, by C. Gregg Singer

The Great Christian Revolution, by Otto Scott

Aspects of Christian Social Ethics, by Carl F.H. Henry

The Collected Works of James M. Buchanan, by James M. Buchanan

American Political Writings During the Founding Era, by Charles S. Hyneman

Lesson 5

The Legacy of John Calvin, by David W. Hall

The Works of John Knox, by John Knox

Constitutionalism and the Separation of Powers, by M.J.C. Vile

Constitutionalism: Ancient and Modern, by Charles Howard McIlwain

Magna Charta: A Commentary on the Great Charter of King John, with a Historical Introduction, by William Sharp McKechni

LAW

&

GOVERNMENT

An Introductory Study Course

Unit One

Unit One–Lesson 1
Building a Theological and Historical Framework

Introduction

When studying the law, ethics, and public policy of nations and other governing institutions in the western world, the Christian statesman enjoys a certain advantage over opposing schools of thought. Scripture provides the Christian with an infallible standard of reference by which to define, analyze, and interpret issues arising in the public square. Moreover, Christianity has dominated the western legal tradition, providing a historical framework firmly rooted in the theology of the Reformation, Christendom, and the Patristic age. In fact, the historical, political framework of the western world cannot be properly studied and understood at all apart from an adequate understanding of its Christian theological and historical foundations.

A mastery of each frame of reference is imperative for the Christian statesman. For instance, a study of the founding documents of the United States of America in light of Christian theology will reveal the Christian foundations of that nation, which, being constituted well over two hundred years ago, represents the oldest existing political system in the world. However, when studied in light of history, the United States of America is one of the most recent expressions of the Christian legal tradition. This unique blend of being both ancient when compared to modern political systems, and modern when studied in light of the historical western tradition makes the United States of America both the oldest and the youngest living representative of the Christian influence on law, ethics, and public policy. This combination has caused some scholars to point out that, "the United States is a surer heir of English Liberties than England, and more deeply rooted in the Christian West than Europe itself."[1] Consequently, this combination makes the United States an ideal modern exemplar of the Christian framework for law, ethics, and public policy in the modern world.

The guiding principles, which gave form to the United States, did not originate out of the intellect or reason of the American founding fathers; rather, America's founders were diligent students of a host of Christian theologians and statesmen who had, through faithful exegesis of Scripture, developed, tested, proved, and championed a definitive Christian framework for law, ethics, and public policy in the Western World for nearly two millennia. If we are to honor the enduring legacy of wisdom, courage, and honor, exhibited by America's founding fathers, it is imperative that we learn to discern issues of law, ethics, and public policy in light of theology and history as they did.

Furthermore, the historical success of the works of our own generation depend on our ability to faithfully and diligently apply the theological framework of the Word of God to every area of life. In the closing of His Sermon on the Mount, Jesus taught:

> *Even so every good tree bringeth forth good fruit; but a corrupt tree bringeth forth evil fruit. A good tree cannot bring forth evil fruit, neither can a corrupt tree bring forth good fruit. Every tree that bringeth not forth good fruit is hewn down, and cast into the fire. Wherefore by their fruits ye shall know them.... Therefore whosoever heareth these sayings of mine, and doeth them, I will liken him unto a wise man, which built his house upon a rock: the rain descended, and the floods came, and the winds blew, and beat upon that house; and it fell not: for it was founded upon a rock. And every one that heareth these sayings of mine, and doeth them not, shall be likened unto a foolish man, which built his house upon the sand: And the rain descended, and the floods came, and the winds blew, and beat upon that house; and it fell: and great was the fall of it.*[2]

This statement also has far-reaching implications with regard to how Christians approach issues of law, ethics, and public policy, discern crucial political issues, and engage the culture around them. The Word of God is the definitive standard by which we are to discern all issues of faith and life. Any human endeavors that are not established firmly on the Word of God are doomed to historical failure from the outset. No solution can bring good fruit and no civil establishment can endure if it compromises, rejects, or contradicts the authority of the Word of God. Whether it is an issue of law, ethics, or public policy a Christian Statesman must learn to practice discernment by looking first to the theological foundations established in Scripture and then, being sensible of its historical fruits, discerning whether they be biblical or unbiblical.

In this lecture, founder and president of Vision Forum, Douglas Phillips, Esq. discusses the surety of America's Christian foundations. He will introduce a variety of topics that demonstrate the failure on the part of many modern Christian Statesmen in discerning matters of law, ethics, and public policy from a theological and historical framework. Finally, he will reveal that the work, intellect, and innovation of man is doomed to certain failure if it is not founded on the Word of God for the purpose of honoring and bringing glory to Him.

Lecture Outline

Introduction to the Christian Foundations of Western Law, Pt. 1

1. John Witherspoon, "The Forgotten Founding Father"

    A. Immigrated from Scotland

    B. President of the College of New Jersey (Preston College of today)

    C. John Adams "He was a true son of Liberty but first he was a son of the cross"

    D. Educator, clergyman, mentor, signed the declaration of Independence

2. The Mission of Witherspoon School of Law

    A. To open the lost book of the Law and to force the antithesis

        i. The importance of God's Word

        ii. Creature-Creator distinctive

        iii. Battle between Satan and the children of promise

        iv. Massacre of children through abortion

        v. The transformation of the legal system from one based on Genesis to an evolving standard (positive law)

        vi. Oliver Wendell Holmes: The most notorious Supreme Court Justice in history, evolutionist, author of the modern Common Law books

  B. To encourage Hebrew education

    i. Modern philosophy of education had its roots in Greek education (the child is the State's; individualistic)

    ii. Hebrew education: The child is a creation of God; member of society, part of the unfolding plan of God; training is relational; first battle in history is over education: God's way vs. man's way

    iii. Doctrine of the Atonement: the concept of restitution, the concept of blood, of the dominion mandate, all association with the Genesis story serves as the definition of the foundation of modern jurisprudence

  C. To prepare men to lead in their family, church, and gates; Proverbs 31; Psalm 127,128

3. The Issue of Absentee Men and Feminism

  A. Isaiah 3:12

  B. Court decision, *Bradwell v. Illinois*

  C. The consideration of a female Chief Executive in our present times

  D. The implications of a "First Lady" to be a man

  E. The Biblical model: man, the protector of women

  F. Alexis de Tocqueville

4. Vulnerability of Being Divided Against Each Other

5. Mentorship, Discipline, and Love

6. Preview of the Issues Covered

  A. What is Law?

  B. Do laws evolve? Do standards change?

  C. Was America founded as a Christian nation?

  D. To what extent is the Constitution Christian?

  E. Who is America's sovereign?

7. Epistemology

  A. Definition: the study of the sources and the limits of human knowledge

  B. William Blackstone: "Law is the rule of action dictated by a superior being"

  C. Can man legislate morality?

    D. Purpose of law to restrain evil

    E. All laws are expressly moral in nature or they are procedure to a moral concept

    F. All men have an object of worship, Romans 1

    G. Van Til "Culture is religion externalized"

    H. Anaximander: c. 610 BC – c. 546 BC was a pre-Socratic Greek philosopher

8. Three Legal Schools of Thought

    A. Rationalism, Evolutionism, Positivism

    B. Semi-Rationalism

    C. Revelationism or theonomic position

9. Inescapable Concepts

    A. Religion

    B. Sovereignty

    C. Faith

    D. Infallibility

10. Fundamental Principles

    A. Law of God is a reflection of the character of God

    B. God doesn't change, His law doesn't change

    C. Creature-Creator distinctive

    D. Sovereignty of God

    E. Great Commission

Questions

1. What influence did John Witherspoon have on America's Founding Fathers?

   _____

   _____

   _____

2. What is the mission of the Witherspoon School of Law?

_____

_____

_____

3. What is the difference between Hebrew and Greek Education?

_____

_____

_____

4. What was the conclusion of the Supreme Court decision in *Bradwell v. Illinois*?

_____

_____

_____

5. Who was the "Superior Being" for the Founding Fathers?

_____

_____

_____

6. What is the purpose of law?

_____

_____

_____

7. Are all men religious?

_____

_____

_____

8. What is the difference between Higher Criticism and Lower Criticism?

_____

_____

_____

9. What are some of the books that John Witherspoon brought with him to America?

_____

_____

_____

10. Which are the four inescapable concepts discussed in this lecture?

_____

_____

_____

Selected Reading

At the Constitutional Convention of 1787, Benjamin Franklin rose and made the following statement concerning the need to carefully lay Christian foundations in the formation of the new Republic:

> *"Mr. President, the small progress we have made after four or five weeks close attendance and continual reasoning with each other— our different sentiments on almost every question, several of the last producing as many noes as ayes, is methinks a melancholy proof of the imperfection of the human understanding. We indeed seem to feel our*

own want of the political wisdom, since we have been running about in search of it. We have gone back to ancient history for models of government, and examined the different forms of those republics which have been formed with the seeds of their own dissolution now no longer exist. And we have viewed Modern States all round Europe, but find none of the their constitutions suitable to our circumstances.

In this situation of this assembly, groping as it were in the dark to find the political truth, and scarce able to distinguish it when presented to us, how has it happened, sir, that we have not hitherto once thought of humbly applying to the Father of Lights to illuminate our understandings? In the beginning of the contest with Great Britain, when we were sensible to danger, we had daily prayers in this room for divine protection. Our prayers, sir, were heard, and they were graciously answered. All of us who were engaged in the struggle must have observed frequent instances of superintending providence in our favor. To that kind providence we owe this happy opportunity of consulting in peace on the means of establishing our future national felicity. And have we now forgotten that powerful friend? Or do we imagine that we no longer need his assistance? I have lived, sir, a long time, and the longer I live, the more convincing proofs I see of this truth – That God governs the affairs of men. And if a sparrow cannot fall to the ground without His notice, is it probable an empire can rise without His aid? We have been assured, sir, in the sacred writings that except the Lord build the house, they labor in vain that build it. I firmly believe this and I also believe that without this concurring aid we shall succeed in this political building no better than the builders of Babel; we shall be divided by our partial little local interests; our projects will be confounded and we ourselves shall become a byword down the future ages. And what is worse, mankind may hereafter, from this unfortunate instance, despair of establishing governments by human wisdom and leave it to chance, war, and conquest." [3]

Definitions

Epistemology: The study of the sources and the limits of human knowledge.

Higher Criticism: The discipline in which men attempt to determine what parts of the Bible are scientifically defensible.

Lower Criticism: A discipline of contrasting the Scripture to detect the actual intent of the Word of God.

Jurisprudence: The science of the law and application of law.

Writing Assignment

English romantic poet, Percy Bysshe Shelley, wrote the following:

> *"I met a traveller from an antique land*
> *who said: "Two vast and trunkless legs of stone*
> *stand in the desert. Near them on the sand,*
> *Half sunk, a shattered visage lies, whose frown*
> *And wrinkled lip and sneer of cold command*
> *Tell that its sculptor well those passions read*
> *Which yet survive, stamped on these lifeless things,*
> *The hand that mocked them and the heart that fed.*
> *And on the pedestal these words appear:*
> *'My name is Ozymandias, King of Kings:*
> *Look on my works, ye mighty, and despair!'*
> *Nothing beside remains. Round the decay*
> *Of that colossal wreck, boundless and bare,*
> *The lone and level sands stretch far away"*

Use what you have learned in this lesson to write at least 500 words about how this poem reflects the true fate of mighty men and nations who are established on foundations without reference to God and His law-word. Conclude by discussing the importance of the Christian foundation in America and what will be the inevitable outcome if the United States continues to abandon that Christian foundation.

Recommendations for Further Study

For You They Signed, by Marilyn Boyer

American History to 1865, by R.J. Rushdoony

Political Sermons of the American Founding Era 1730-1805 (2 Vols.), Editor, Ellis Sandoz

Christianity and the American Commonwealth: The Influence of Christianity in Making This Nation, by Charles B. Galloway D.D, LL.D.

Christianity in the United States, by Daniel Dorchester

Christian Life & Character of the Civil Institutions of the United States, by Benjamin F. Morris

Unit One–Lesson 2
Biblical Worldview and Christian Statesmanship

Introduction

While secular humanism has groped in the dark for just over a century to establish even the slightest semblance of law, justice, and order, Christianity has advanced a definitive standard of law, ethics, and public policy in the civil realm for over two millennia. Modernly, much has been said about the establishment of common ground between these two traditions in matters of law, ethics, and public policy. The idea that there can be common ground between Christians and non-Christians is not a new concept at all; the Bible provides a very definitive framework for commonality between Christians and non-Christians in the public square. Commonality, is biblically achieved by acknowledging, as did America's founding fathers, that we are all created in the image of God and created for His glory alone, that we are all commanded to follow the same standard of righteousness and that we will all stand before the same judgment seat to give account for what we did and did not do. Yet, this is the very thing that unbelievers tend to require Christians to reject, or at least keep quiet about, if they are to be welcomed in the public square.

Sadly, a large number of those called by the name of Christ have denied the Authority of God over the civil realm and abandoned the long established biblical standards for civil government. Modern Christians have slowly grown accepting of the call for secular "non-religious" political institutions. This general acceptance among Christians of the secular "non-religious" framework as a framework for commonality in the public square has been devastating. Every political system is built on certain basic faith assumptions about what is ultimate in the universe. Once the ultimate is determined a standard of ethics is developed to serve the will of the ultimate. Finally, that standard of ethics is applied to every area of life through a system of law, ethics, and public policy.

The question is not whether or not politics and faith mix. Rather, the question is who has more integrity and veracity in applying the faith they have to the world in which they live (i.e. Who will take their faith more seriously?). Christians who profess the authority of Christ over matters of personal salvation and the church, but deny His absolute authority over the political realm are in fact professing that humanistic faith is more reliable in matters of law, ethics, and public policy. In effect, many professing Christians have willingly made the same profession toward modern pagans, that a number of ancient pagans were forced to make when they bore witness to the mighty hand of God, "your god, he is God."[4] The acceptance of the humanistic framework of a secular "non-religious" state is a denial of God and His sovereignty over His creation.

Some Christians have argued that we live in a pluralistic culture in which the Christian influence is just one among many schools of thought in which we must seek to make significant contributions to the political system overall. The attempt of many to accept the idea of pluralism as a legitimate paradigm is a rejection of the one true God in favor of a system in which multiple deities coexist as equals. In effect, pluralism is a profession of polytheism as being authoritative over the civil realm. In essence, it is a rejection of the total sovereign authority of God over all matters of political and legal significance and an acceptance of the sovereignty of man to be able to borrow from many different sources as deemed appropriate by unaided reason. According to pluralism, God is not a sovereign, but rather one advisor among many to the sovereignty of man in the political sphere.

Christians have been given a sacred commission to teach the nations to observe all those things that Christ taught. If they are to fulfill their great commission, they must boldly assert the counsel of God in issues of law, ethics, and public policy in the face of strong opposition and ridicule. In part two of this lecture Doug Phillips Esq. will confront these common trends of compromise among Christians in the public square. He will explain how the Christian statesman can guard against the common traps of compromise that snare so many professing Christians in the public sphere. Finally, he explains that the testimony of Scripture is absolutely essential to issues of law, ethics, and public policy, and that faith in God is the sole basis for wisdom and rationality.

Lecture Outline

Introduction to the Christian Foundations of Western Law, Pt. 2

1. The God of the Copy Book Headings

    A. Modernity literate in marketplace trends but illiterate of the Law of God

    B. Many modern Christians are ashamed of the Gospel in the public square

2. Christians Must Learn to Think and Reason by the Word of God

    A. Christians must provide answers from the biblical foundations

    B. Christians must examine the extent they are immersed in pagan culture

    C. The Desert Island Challenge

3. Christians Must Learn to be Epistemologically Self-conscious

4. The Scripture Must be Our Only Standard for All Faith and Life

    A. Christians must be dedicated to the study of Scripture

    B. Christians must be dedicated to prayer

5. Christians Must Acknowledge the Sovereign Authority of God Over All Things

    A. God is the starting point of all rationality and proper reason

    B. All knowledge and wisdom is deposited in Christ

6. Human Reason Unaided by Reference to God is Insufficient

    A. The Creature and Creator Distinctive

    B. Human emotions and senses are not the standard of truth

7. Christians Must Learn to Think Presuppositionally

    A. The revelation of God is supreme in the interpretation of experiences and facts

B. Human reason must be brought into subjection to Christ

C. Experience is a confirmation process of revelation and reason

8. Christian Faith is Essential to Rationality

A. Transcendence

B. Rationalism

C. Fideism

9. The Importance of a Proper Framework for Apologetics

A. The Sufficiency of Scripture

B. Pop Quiz

10. Common Mis-readings of Scripture

A. Cultural misconceptions and false maxims concerning Scripture must be avoided

11. The Implications of God's Law

A. First, the Law asserts principles

B. Second, the Law cites cases as illustrations of those principles

C. Third, the Law aims at the restitution of God's order.

12. The Law of God Must be Seen in Light of its Divisions

A. Laws of personal morality

B. Laws of social interaction

C. Laws of abrogated ceremony

Questions

1. Why have modern Christians failed to influence the public square to the extent former generations of Christians influenced the public square?

_____

_____

_____

2. What does it mean to be epistemologically self-conscious?

_____

_____

_____

3. Why is it important to the Christian statesman to be given to fervent prayer and diligent reading of Scripture in order to have a right view of law, ethics, and public policy?

_____

_____

_____

4. What does it mean to put on the mind of Christ?

_____

_____

_____

5. Why does the Creator-Creature distinction debunk the idea of pluralism?

_____

_____

_____

6. What does it mean that the Scripture is sufficient?

_____

_____

_____

7. Why is fideism contrary to a Christian view of epistemology?

_____

_____

_____

8. Why are maxims and misconceptions of Scripture dangerous?

_____

_____

_____

9. How is the commandment, "thou shalt not muzzle the ox while he treads out the corn" applied by Paul?

_____

_____

_____

10. What three traditional categories can the law of God be divided into?

_____

_____

_____

Selected Reading

In his farewell address, George Washington, stated the following about the indispensable nature of America's Christian foundations:

> "Of all the dispositions and habits, which lead to political prosperity, Religion and Morality are indispensable supports. In vain would that man claim the tribute of Patriotism, who should labor to subvert these great pillars of human happiness, these firmest props of the duties of Men and Citizens. The mere Politician, equally with the pious man,

ought to respect and to cherish them. A volume could not trace all their connections with private and public felicity. Let it simply be asked, Where is the security for property, for reputation, for life, if the sense of religious obligation desert the oaths, which are the instruments of investigation in Courts of Justice? And let us with caution indulge the supposition, that morality can be maintained without religion. Whatever may be conceded to the influence of refined education on minds of peculiar structure, reason and experience both forbid us to expect, that national morality can prevail in exclusion of religious principle.

It is substantially true, that virtue or morality is a necessary spring of popular government. The rule, indeed, extends with more or less force to every species of free government. Who, that is a sincere friend to it, can look with indifference upon attempts to shake the foundation of the fabric?"

Definitions

Antithesis: The rhetorical contrast of ideas by means of a contradictory anti-thesis asserted over against a thesis.

Presupposition: The most basic faith assumptions in one's reasoning by which everything is interpreted and evaluated in the process by which opinions are formed.

Transcendence: Something that exists outside of man's experience.

Fideism: The belief that faith is practiced notwithstanding that faith may be unreasonable.

Epistemology: The study of the nature, source, and limits of human knowledge.

Writing Assignment

During the early persecutions of the church under Rome a controversy arose regarding what to do with those individuals who denied the Christian faith under threat of persecution and then later desired to rejoin the church. Under the Emperor Valerian, a persecution arose when Christians refused to make sacrifices to the Romans gods, as required by law. Citizens were required to carry certificates of proof that they had offered the required sacrifices. Some Christians illegally purchased certificates to avoid persecution, while others fearing for their lives offered the sacrifice required by law. The Churches struggled with what to do with those who had recanted Christ, but who desired to remain members of the church. Those who had purchased certificates to avoid persecution were placed under church discipline and later admitted to fellowship. Yet those who had recanted and offered the sacrifice were welcomed back into the church, but many were never readmitted to the Lord's table. Modernly, in the same way many Christians who hold civil office profess Christ over matters of private faith, but deny the authority of Christ over the public square because they are ashamed of the gospel. Worse, while early Christians feared being torn apart by lions or burned alive, modern Christians deny Christ in fear of being thought foolish and losing face. Considering what you have learned in this lesson, write at least 500 words describing how the early church might have handled Christians in influential positions who denied the authority of Christ in matters of law and public policy. Also, compare the success of the early church in influencing their culture in the midst of persecution to the influence of modern Christians who enjoy religious liberty.

Recommendations for Further Study

Foundations of Christians Scholarship, Editor, Gary North

Always Ready, by Greg Bahnsen

The Sufficiency of Scripture, by Joseph Stephen

Knowing Scripture, R.C. Sproul

Myths, Lies, and Half Truths, by Gary DeMar

Defending the Christian Worldview Against All Opposition, Series 1 & 2, by Greg Bahnsen

A Refutation of Pluralism, by John Brown of Haddington

Unit One–Lesson 3
Creation, Sovereignty, and Providence

Introduction

Society's view of origins is central to its view of law, ethics, and public policy. Basic faith assumptions regarding origins will determine questions about who is sovereign, what the nature of man is, what man's relationship to his community is, and whether law is fixed and transcendent or a local evolving process. The Scripture teaches that God created the world in six, twenty-four hour days, which establishes that God is sovereign over all of His creation, that man is a creature and bound to define every aspect of his community according to the prerogatives of God, and that law is fixed and transcendent over every aspect of creation. Although Charles Darwin is not known as a legal theorist, his view of origins was based on the already popular social evolution of Hegel. Charles Darwin did not go to nature as a neutral observer, but merely applied the already accepted social evolution of Hegel to nature.[5] Under this theory of origins, man is sovereign over a random and thoroughly chaotic universe, man is an animal bound by local social conventions established by groups of men, and like nature, law is a local ever-evolving procession of social norms.

The question of origins is ultimately important to issues of law, ethics, and public policy, because it will determine who is the sovereign and lawgiver of that society. A sovereign provides the basis for human rights and will determine the nature, extent, and security of those rights. Therefore, if God is the sovereign of a nation, our rights are establish by Him and are unalienable against any other power. If the sovereign is human reason as expressed through a nation state, our rights are ultimately established by the state and alienable by the highest court in the land according to the state's interest. This delineation with regard to sovereignty provides the most vital contrast between the worldview of America's founders and the worldview of those in positions of civil power in the United States today. The Declaration of Independence issued collectively by the United States declares, " [men] are endowed by their Creator with certain unalienable rights."[6] Yet, modern courts have stripped the rights of citizens by limiting them according to a "compelling state interest." This difference ultimately reflects more than a change in public policy, but a change in the view of sovereignty.

John Calvin and Charles Darwin are crucially important figures in the war of origins and in the ultimate battle between claims for sovereignty. While these men lived centuries apart and they are virtually juxtaposed in every way, they have one basic similarity; the work of each man is known for popularizing a particular view of sovereignty. John Calvin championed the sovereignty of God, while Charles Darwin championed the sovereignty of the natural man. All standards of law, ethics, and public policy may be delineated by these two views: origins and sovereignty. It is crucially important for the Christian statesman to understand by these claims of sovereignty that law, ethics, and public policy are inescapably religious in nature. Many Christian statesmen involved in the political process attempt to shy away from giving the appearance of being overly influenced by Christian faith to avoid being accused of forcing their religious views onto the rest of society. Yet, the legislation of law is a matter of forcing a particular standard of morality on society whether they agree with the legislation or not.

The secularist, claiming religious neutrality, imposes a wicked standard of morality on the rest of the population when laws are passed which force Christian commercial real estate owners to rent commercial space to immoral institutions or to rent residential space to an unmarried couple. A standard of morality is forced on the rest of society when mandatory taxes are raised to fund the killing of children through abortions. What Christians must ultimately understand is that morality will by its very nature be imposed on the rest of society whether they agree or not, but who's morality is to be enforced will ultimately be determined by the question of sovereignty. While churches are not vested with the right, or even the ability, to force individuals to convert to Christianity, Christians in the public sphere, in recognizing that God and not man is sovereign, must advance God's prerogatives for law, ethics, and public policy in the public square regardless of a national consensus. In the advancement of the sovereignty of God in the public square, man's consent is not required, because God alone, and not man, is sovereign.

The Christian statesman must, from the outset, determine who holds the ultimate claim of sovereignty over his view of law, ethics, and public policy. In this lecture, Doug Phillip, Esq. will expound on the contrasts that exist between the Calvinistic and the Darwinian positions. Moreover, he will discuss the impact that each thesis has had on the development of Western law.

Lecture Outline

Genesis to Geneva: The Emergence of Liberty in the West

1. The Importance of Genesis

    A. Atonement

    B. Doctrine of restitution

    C. Foundations of Law and civilization

2. John Calvin

    A. Articulated the theology, the philosophy, and the outworking of the reformation doctrine as applied to nations, church, and family.

    B. The school of Geneva

    C. Representative Government

    D. The importance of the Geneva Bible

3. The Doctrine of the Atonement: Our Basic Construct for Western Jurisprudence

    A. God is just and requires death for the breaking of His law

4. Basic Concepts of Legal Theory Found in Genesis, Pentateuch, and Elaborated in Common Law

    A. Jurisdiction

    B. Equality

    C. Fault

  D. Vow

  E. Dominion

  F. Restitution

5. Jurisdiction (Family, Church, State)

  A. Each jurisdiction has privileges, responsibilities, and sanctions

6. Equality

  A. Equal application of the Law

  B. The civil magistrate is under the law

7. Fault

  A. Intent

8. Restitution

  A. The purpose of the law is to restore the criminal, to satisfy God's justice and to make the victim whole.

  B. Death penalty is merciful in God's economy

9. Dominion Mandate

  A. Expression of the absolute sovereignty and lordship of Christ

  B. There is no area in which we are not to take dominion

  C. Great Commission, discipleship

10. The Basic Foundation for Western Law

  A. Criminal Law

  B. Tort Law (the law of personal injury)

  C. The laws of Evidence

  D. Real and personal Property Law

  E. Contract Law

  F. Constitutional Law

  G. Civil Procedure

11. Evidence and Procedure

A. Derived from Scripture

B. Two witnesses are required in capital cases

C. The need of procedure justice and substantive justice

12. The Doctrine of Providence

A. The Westminster Confessions of Faith

B. All creation is under the providence of God

13. Law and Earth History

A. Themes of first millennium

    i. Creation: God is the sovereign

    ii. Commission

    iii. Fall of man

    iv. Curse, judgment

    v. Hope of liberty and freedom by faith in the Redeemer

B. Second and third millennium: Judicial judgment on the earth

C. Third, fourth century

    i. God's covenant with His people

    ii. Laws

    iii. The establishment of the Hebrew Republic

D. Sixth millennium: The work of the Reformation vs. Renaissance

E. Present day: Evolution, statism, transformation of the family and the battle over authority

14. Common Law

A. Christian from its origins: The case laws of Moses

B. Principles of the *Magna Charta*

Questions

1. Where do we discover the first foundations of law and civilization?

_____

_____

_____

2. What biblical doctrine lays the foundation for the American doctrine of jurisprudence?

_____

_____

_____

3. What are the basic concepts of legal theory found in Genesis, the Pentateuch, and elaborated in Common Law?

_____

_____

_____

4. What is the purpose of criminal law according to God's Word?

_____

_____

_____

5. What are the seven basic foundations for Western Law?

_____

_____

_____

6. According to the Westminster Confessions of Faith what is meant by the Doctrine of Providence?

_____

_____

_____

7. How many witnesses were required in the Scripture to put an offender to death? Two witnesses were required.

_____

_____

_____

8. What is the legal doctrine of subpoena?

_____

_____

_____

9. What is the difference between Procedural Law and Substantive Law?

_____

_____

_____

10. What influence does the *Magna Charta* have on the United States?

_____

_____

_____

Selected Reading

In the following selection, founding father to America's Founding Fathers, John Witherspoon, speaks of the nature of divine providence as it is exercised over unbelievers in a sermon titled, *The Dominion of Providence over the passions of Men*:

> "There is not a greater evidence either of the reality or the power of religion, than a firm belief of God's universal presence, and a constant attention to the influence and operation of his providence. It is by this means that the Christian may be said, in the emphatical scripture language, 'to walk with God, and to endure as seeing him who is invisible.'
>
> The doctrine of divine providence is very full and complete in the sacred oracles. It extends not only to things which we may think of great moment, and therefore worthy of notice, but to things the most indifferent and inconsiderable; 'Are not two sparrows sold for a farthing,' says our Lord, 'and one of them falleth not to the ground without your heavenly Father;' nay, 'the very hairs of your head are all numbered.['] It extends not only to things beneficial and salutary, or to the direction and assistance of those who are the servants of the living God; but to things seemingly most hurtful and destructive, and to persons the most refractory and disobedient. He overrules all his creatures, and all their actions. Thus we are told, that 'fire, hail, snow, vapour, and stormy wind, fulfil his word,' in the course of nature; and even so the most impetuous and disorderly passions of men, that are under no restraint from themselves, are yet perfectly subject to the dominion of Jehovah. They carry his commission, they obey his orders, they are limited and restrained by his authority, and they conspire with every thing else in promoting his glory. There is the greater need to take notice of this, that men are not generally sufficiently aware of the distinction between the law of God and his purpose; they are apt to suppose, that as the temper of the sinner is contrary to the one, so the outrages of the sinner are able to defeat the other; than which nothing can be more false. The truth is plainly asserted, and nobly expressed by the psalmist in the text, 'Surely the wrath of man shall praise thee; the remainder of wrath shalt thou restrain.'"

Definitions

Providence: That God as the Creator governs all creatures, actions, and things by His most wise and holy providence according to His infallible foreknowledge and the free and immutable council of His own will for His own glory.

Restitution: The act of restoring a victim to the condition he would have been in had he not been victimized by a criminal.

Capital Punishment: The highest civil sanction of taking a criminal's life.

Writing Assignment

The doctrines of Creation, Sovereignty, and Providence naturally flow from one another. Because God created the world it naturally follows that He would be sovereign over it. If God is sovereign then it naturally follows that He orchestrates the affairs of His creation through providence. There are many modern theological schools that reject the biblical view of God's sovereignty and providence; instead, they place the course of human events on the reason, choice, and actions of man. These schools are very similar to rationalists. While professing to believe in the existence of God and even His sovereignty, this school of thought holds that man is ultimately the determining factor on how God's will is ultimately concluded in matters of salvation and matters of the civil realm. Therefore, God is sovereign, but man ultimately has a veto power over the manner in which God's will is demonstrated in matters of salvation and in matters of law, ethics, and public policy in the civil realm. In light of this lesson, write a 500-word essay on why a biblical doctrine of providence essential to our legal system and how these schools of thought lead to drastically different outcomes in terms of an approach to Christian Statesmanship. Read the Westminster Confession of Faith and discuss some of the practical implications that it should have on you personally as a Christian statesman.

Recommendations for Further Study

The Genevan Reformation and the American Founding, by David W. Hall

God, Man, and Law: the Biblical Principles, by Herbert W. Titus

Lex Rex, by Samuel Rutherford

The Roots of the American Republic, by E.C. Wines

Sovereignty, by R.J. Rushdoony

Unit One–Lesson 4
The Supremacy of Scripture

Introduction

The canon of Scripture is the rule of faith within the Christian worldview. The doctrines of the authority, sufficiency, and inerrancy of scripture are central to what the Christian claims to know about God and his relations with the universe. The word *canon* is from the Latin word *kanon*, which means a straight rod used as a ruler.[7] In the same manner, the Westminster Confession speaks of the Canon of Scripture as being "given by inspiration of God, to be the rule for faith and life."[8] Therefore, God has given the canon of Scripture not only to govern matters of salvation, but as a rule for every aspect of life and thought. The only alternative to this infallible divine standard for all of life is a fallible humanistic standard for all of life. The denial of the authority, sufficiency, and inerrancy of Scripture over every aspect of life inevitably leads to humanistic legalism.

Many view legalism as too strict an adherence to God's Law, but this in itself is an expression of the type of legalism that Scripture warns against. For instance, the legalism of the Pharisees was not that they were too strict in their adherence to the Law of God, but rather that they had replaced it with their own laws and tradition. Jesus warned:

> *"Whosoever therefore shall break one of these least commandments, and shall teach men so, he shall be called the least in the kingdom of heaven: but whosoever shall do and teach them, the same shall be called great in the kingdom of heaven. For I say unto you, that except your righteousness shall exceed the righteousness of the scribes and Pharisees, ye shall in no case enter into the kingdom of heaven."* [9]

Instead, the legalism of the Pharisees was the fact that they made the law of God of no effect through their traditions and social norms.[10] The leaven of the Pharisees was not their use of the law of God, but rather their hypocrisy toward it.[11] Therefore, legalism in the biblical sense of the word is denying the relevance of God's law word and replacing it with the laws, traditions, and modern social norms of man.

"Culture is simply the service of God in our lives; it is religion externalized."[12] The rule of faith in a nation will also be the rule for law, ethics, and public policy. Christian faith is not merely something that Christians profess to believe, but it is fundamental to every aspect of life and thought. To claim to have faith toward God and hold to His rule for faith and life, yet, deny God's sovereignty over the civil realm, or to deny Scripture as the only standard for law, ethics, and public policy is a form of pharisaical legalism and hypocrisy. The Christian statesman must learn to avoid this form of legalism by, first, acknowledging that Scripture is not only a rule for matters of faith, but is also a rule for all of life, and second to reject the laws, traditions, and social norms of men, and recognize God's law word as the only rule for law, ethics, and public policy in the civil realm.

There are a number of areas in which the traditions and social norms of our modern age come into direct conflict with the Scripture. Sadly, in many of these areas Christians have not been diligent in providing biblical answers to these issues, but instead have allowed these issues and themselves to be guided by the humanistic traditions and social norms and not by the law of God. In this symposium, William Einwecter and Doug Phillips will address a number of these conflicts and will answer hard questions with regard to how Christians are to respond to these conflicts in a distinctly biblical manner.

Lecture Outline

Symposium on the Reformation and Law

1. Sin Complicates, but Righteousness Simplifies

2. Doctrine of Women

3. Military

    A. Homosexuality

    B. Women

    C. Unjustifiable warfare

4. How to Honor the Law of the Land Without Violating Scripture

5. Voting

    A. The ability to write in candidates in our democratic republic

    B. We can never vote for someone that is biblically unqualified

    C. Women are not biblically qualified to hold public office

    D. More important that few people do well than many do bad: Lot's family example

    E. The Church of Jesus Christ is the object of God's love and the true centerpiece of history

6. Biblical Law in Secular Debates

    A. Following the example of Paul in Acts 17

        i. Declares the ignorance of the individuals

        ii. Appeals to the doctrine of creation

        iii. Call to repentance

    B. We are witnesses for Jesus Christ in every public debate

    C. "Socrates or Christ": Greg Bahnsen, *Foundations of Christian Scholarship*

    D. Faulty arguments and man's reasoning

Questions

1. What is the debate over every issue of life?

_____

_____

_____

2. What are some problems facing men in military?

_____

_____

_____

3. If we make Jesus Christ the center of our lives in the field of employment what should our expectations be?

_____

_____

_____

4. Should women hold civil office based on Scripture?

_____

_____

_____

5. What can we learn from the example of Lot's family?

_____

_____

_____

6. Can we, in good conscience, vote for someone who is biblically unqualified?

_____

_____

_____

7. What is the centerpiece of history?

_____

_____

_____

8. What is the model in Scriptures used for debating with non-Christians?

_____

_____

_____

9. What is the pattern Paul uses in the debate?

_____

_____

_____

10. In the public sphere, what should we always have in mind while debating?

_____

_____

_____

Further Reading

The *Mayflower Compact* is a social covenant among Christian men of faith which express their intention to be governed by a civil establishment under Christian faith:

> *"In the name of God, Amen. We whose names are under-written, the loyal subjects of our dread sovereign Lord, King James, by the grace of God, of Great Britain, France, and Ireland King, Defender of the Faith, etc.*
>
> *Having undertaken, for the glory of God, and advancement of the Christian faith, and honor of our King and Country, a voyage to plant*

the first colony in the northern parts of Virginia, do by these present solemnly and mutually, in the presence of God, and one of another, covenant and combine our selves together into a civil body politic, for our better ordering and preservation and furtherance of the ends aforesaid; and by virtue hereof to enact, constitute, and frame such just and equal laws, ordinances, acts, constitutions and offices, from time to time, as shall be thought most meet and convenient for the general good of the Colony, unto which we promise all due submission and obedience. In witness whereof we have hereunder subscribed our names at Cape Cod, the eleventh of November, in the year of the reign of our sovereign lord, King James, of England, France, and Ireland, the eighteenth, and of Scotland the fifty-fourth. Anno Dom. 1620."

Definitions

Commonwealth: An aggregate of independent governments loosely organized for the good of all.

Just War Theory: The idea that in order for a nation to be ethically justified in going to war against another nation they must have biblical provocation.

Writing Assignment

Henry Van Til wrote that culture is religion externalized. In other words, the culture will reflect the predominant faith of the people of that culture. Some professing Christian scholars have looked on the idea of a Christian culture with suspicion, and some have even stated that Christian culture could never exist since it would require everyone to be Christian. Of course, such a notion would deny that any culture could exist since no culture can claim a universal uniformity of social ethics. One such enemy of Christian culture, Anabaptist scholar Leonard Verduin, rejects the idea of what he calls "sacral society" which he defines as a "society held together by a religion to which all members of that society are committed."[13] Of course, during the founding era, America was what Verduin would decry as a "Sacral society" since at that time 98.4% of the population were professing Christians. The Christian religion was the predominate influence that held all men and society together. It is only to be expected that the predominate faith of a culture will influence every aspect of social integration and that citizens would strive to enjoy the protections and the benefits promised in Scripture for nations who acknowledge the sovereignty of God. Write a 500-word essay describing some of the practical aspects of a Christian culture that thoroughly applied the word of God to every aspect of their social interactions. Discuss how such a society would differ from American culture today.

Recommendations for Further Study

Thinking Straight in a Crooked World, by Gary DeMar

The Shape of Sola Scriptura, by Keith Matheson

The Canon of Scripture, by F.F. Bruce

The Calvinistic Concept of Culture, by Henry Van Til

Sola Scriptura: The Protestant Position on the Bible, Editor, Joel R. Beeke

Unit Two

Unit Two–Lesson 1
The Importance of the Biblical Doctrine of Jurisdiction

Introduction

Before He ascended into heaven and sat down at the right hand of the Father, Jesus told His disciples, "All power is given unto me in heaven and in earth."[14] There is not a single aspect of God's creation over which Jesus has not been made both Lord and Christ. [15] Jurisdiction involves the right to speak with authority to a certain issue within a certain geographical boundary. Therefore, since all authority has been given to Christ and the boundaries of that authority extend to all of heaven and all of earth, there is no true authority on earth apart from Christ. When Jesus is called King of kings and Lord of lords, it is not merely an honorary title, but rather it is a declarative of His complete jurisdiction and authority. There is no authority which falls outside of the total dominion of Christ.

Therefore, all authority is derivative from Christ. An individual's obligation to obey a higher authority is based on the obligation of all men to obey Christ. This also means that no authority is absolute, but rather all authority is limited to the authority that God has prescribed. There are only three delegations of authority, to which men have an obligation to obey: the civil government, the church government, and the family government. Each of these is limited with respect to authority and each is exclusive from one another. When one form of government exerts power that is outside of the authority given by Christ or interferes with the authority of another form of government it is an act of tyranny.

This biblical idea of a jurisdictional form of limited civil government was written into the United States Constitution. First of all the United States Constitution limits the powers of the Federal government to those duties that are specified in the constitution itself. All other power, the great majority of the power, was reserved to the states. When the federal government takes actions that exceed the authority provided in the United States Constitution it is an act of tyranny. Secondly, it is an important point to make that, despite what it has modernly held itself out to be, the United States is not a nation. The United States is a constitutionally federated union of independent republican states. The preamble of the Constitution specifies what the thirteen independent states were hoping to achieve. These were to "form a more perfect Union, establish Justice, ensure domestic tranquility, provide for the common defense, promote the general welfare, and secure the blessings of liberty to ourselves and our posterity, to ordain and establish this Constitution for the United States of America." It was clear at the time that the Constitution was drafted that the federal government was being constituted to be an inferior to serve the interests of the thirteen independent states. This federal system was one based on the biblical concept of limited jurisdictions. Thirdly, the United States divided the Federal Government into three distinct branches to carry out different functions and act as checks and balances to their branches of Government. Again, this was also based on the biblical concept of jurisdiction and limited government.

Consequently, one of the most important questions that a Christian statesman can learn to ask with regard to law, ethics, and public policy is by what standard? By what standard (i.e. by what authority) may a particular form of government compel men toward a particular action? When the actions of any form of government are examined and found to exceed the authority or jurisdictional boundaries given to it by Christ, it is an act of tyranny.

In this lecture, William Einwecter goes to Scripture to show the biblical framework for the doctrine of jurisdiction. He will also explain the covenantal nature of jurisdictional authority and the consequences of tyranny that befall a nation that has forgotten the law of God.

Lecture Outline

Covenantal Approach to Jurisdiction

1. The Fundamental Questions of Government: Luke 20:1-2

    A. By what authority?

    B. Do you have jurisdiction?

2. Deuteronomy 21:1-3

    A. The basic principle of Scripture: God's Law must be administered by the proper jurisdiction

3. Christian Doctrine of Government and Jurisdiction

    A. Psalm 47:2,6,7,8

    B. The mediatorial kingship of Christ: Philippians 3:9-11, Acts 3:32-36, Daniel 7:13-14, Psalm 2:6-12

    C. The authority of God's Law: Deuteronomy 6:17, Ecclesiastes 12:13-14

    D. Self-Government: Romans 14:10-12

        1. Liberty of conscience

4. Family, Church, and State Government

    A. Institution: an organization or a group of persons that has been founded for particular purposes

    B. Separate governments and covenantal institutions

5. The Biblical Covenant Model

    A. Transcendence, Hierarchy, Ethics, Oaths & Sanctions (Abraham example), Succession

    B. The spheres of government are based on and dependent on self-government

    C. There is a definite institutional separation between the three spheres of government

    D. There is an interdependence between the three spheres of government

    E. All three spheres of government are necessary for a well-ordered human society

    F. None of these governing institutions are monolithic

G. God uses each sphere of government to promote obedience to His Law and punish transgressions of it

6. Liberty and Government

A. Joseph's example

Questions

1. Are the questions asked by the priests and scribes in Luke 20:1-2 legitimate?

_____

_____

_____

2. What are the fundamental questions of Government?

_____

_____

_____

3. What is the basic principle of the application of Scripture?

_____

_____

_____

4. What is meant by the kingship of Christ?

_____

_____

_____

5. How does God govern His creation?

_____

_____

_____

6. By what standard does Jesus govern the nations?

_____

_____

_____

7. According to the London Baptist Confession, what does liberty of conscience mean?

_____

_____

_____

8. What does self-maledictory oath mean?

_____

_____

_____

9. What are the elements of the biblical covenantal model?

_____

_____

_____

10. Which sphere of government is most important?

_____

_____

_____

Further Reading

One of America's leading influencers in the cause for independence, Samuel Adams, wrote the following poem concerning the source of all liberty[16]:

> "All temporal power is of God, And the magistratal, His institution, laud, to but advance creaturely happiness aubaud:
>
> Let us then affirm the Source of Liberty.
>
> Ever agreeable to nature and will, Of the Supreme and Guardian of all yet still Employed for our rights and freedom's thrill:
>
> Thus proves the only Source of Liberty.
>
> Though our civil joy is surely expressed Through the hearth, and home, and church manifest, Yet this too shall be a nation's true test:
>
> To acknowledge the divine Source of Liberty."

Definitions

Malediction: The act of calling down a curse that invokes evil

Monolithic: An organization or system that is large, powerful, indivisible, and slow to change.

Jurisdiction: Latin word *juris* means of right, of law; and *diction* means to speak, declare; so jurisdiction means the right to speak concerning certain things or to certain areas of life.

Sanhedrin: The ruling counsel of Israel formed by the priests, the scribes, and the elders.

Writing Assignment

The English Civil War under Oliver Cromwell was often said to be a war to restore the rights of Englishmen to those they enjoyed prior to the totalitarian rise of Norman law. Yet after Cromwell's death, the temporary restoration of the tyranny of the Stuart kings led to the Glorious Revolution. However, one failure of the Glorious Revolution is that it reflected the writings of its chief philosopher, John Locke. Instead of a restoration of jurisdictional liberty, as Cromwell had proposed, the Glorious Revolution merely transferred the power of the King to "the people" as represented in Parliament. William Blackstone pointed out that under English law, if Parliament enacted an unreasonable law, there was no Constitution that is vested with the authority to restrain it. The end result of this problem is illustrated by a statement made by English Attorney General, Sir Hartley Shawcross, in 1946, who said, "Parliament is sovereign; it may make any laws. It could ordain that all blue-eyed babies be destroyed at birth." [17] Write an essay of at least 500 words describing the vital importance of the doctrine of Jurisdiction in opposing totalitarian governments. Include a discussion about what you think England might have been like if this biblical doctrine would have remained in place after the death of Oliver Cromwell.

Recommendations for Further Study

This Independent Republic, by R.J. Rushdoony

Messiah the Prince, by William Symington

God and Government, by Gary DeMar

By This Standard, by Greg Bahnsen

Unit Two–Lesson 2
A Separation of Church and State

Introduction

When the phrase separation of church and state is used it can signify a number of ideologies. When many speak of the separation of church and state, including modern American jurisprudence, they mean that the civil government is forbidden from taking actions that are considered religious in nature. Still others would use it to mean the existence of a civil government that is directed and controlled by a church. Yet, it may surprise most people that the separation of church and state was built into the federal government on the basis of religious, and not secular, considerations. Moreover, what America's founding fathers understood by a separation of church and state is worlds apart from what many understand the phrase to mean today.

God has established two distinct jurisdictions of church and state, each with separate and independent spheres of government. Neither has sovereignty over the other, both are equally ultimate in their own spheres of authority, and Christ alone is the head of each.[18] "To admit that the church is separated from the state is not the same as saying that the state is separated from obligations to God Himself and His Rule", reformed scholar Greg Bahnsen pointed out. "Both church and state as separate institutions with separate functions (i.e. The church mercifully ministers the gospel, while the state justly ministers public law by the sword.), serve under the authority of God, the Creator, Sustainer, King, and Judge of all mankind in all aspects of their lives." [19] With this understanding, America's founders never imagined that the civil government could sever itself from the rule of God and expect success or lasting prosperity.

America's founders were dealing with a problem that had carried over from England. Since the reign of Henry VIII of England, the kings of England had held themselves out to be the head of the church as well as the head of civil government. This was a clear violation of the biblical separation of church and state. Later, the same union of church and state were established in colonies like Virginia, which early on led to a struggle for religious liberty. Churches in Virginia were required to ask the civil government for permission to exist, which only granted permission to the established Anglican Church and a few Presbyterian Congregations. Those who preached the gospel without a license were jailed. Only marriages administered in licensed churches were recognized as valid. Taxes were levied to fund the ministry of the church, so that Presbyterians and Baptists were in effect required to pay a double tithe. Reformed Baptist and Presbyterian churches who understood the biblical separation of church and state were at the forefront of a struggle that led to the disestablishment of the state licensure of churches in Virginia; that ultimately lead to the adoption of the First Amendment to the United States Constitution.

The First Amendment to the United States Constitution only applied to the federal congress and was not intended to apply to the independent states. Those who fought for the disestablishment of the Anglican churches in Virginia did not view the first amendment as means to impose a disestablishment on the remaining twelve colonies; that was something that the United States Constitution by its very nature did not have the power or authority to do. Rather, the First Amendment to the United States Constitution was intended to place a restriction on the United States Congress from attempting to impose a specific state religion on the independent states or to prohibit a legitimate religious exercise.

The First amendment is not, nor can it be, a restriction on churches or religious individuals, nor does it prohibit a Christian Statesman's obedience to God in the public square. The First Amendment is merely a prohibition of the United States Congress from meddling with those things that are within the exclusive jurisdiction of the church. In this lecture, Doug Phillips will discuss the biblical doctrine of separation of church and state. Furthermore, he will expound on the history of the separation of church and state and dispel the modern misunderstandings of the doctrine.

Lecture Outline

1. **George Gillespie: *Aaron's Rod Blossoming***

   A. The correlation to the Bible

   B. Aaron's rod: A symbol of authority, and the blessing of God on the authority figure

2. **Erastianism**

   A. Placed the supremacy of the State over the Church.

3. **Catholic Model**

   A. The Papal Revolution

   B. The Catholic model placed the Church's authority over the State and Family

4. **The Reformed View of the Three Jurisdictions**

   A. Each jurisdiction has its own roles with little overlapping

   B. Each jurisdiction is under God

   C. One does not have preeminence over the other

5. **Symbols of Enforcement**

   A. The Family-the rod of correction

   B. The Church-the keys

   C. The State-the sword

6. **Examples of Jurisdictions**

7. **Limitations and Boundaries**

8. **Westminster Assembly**

   A. George Gillespie's message in the "Great Debate"

   B. Secured the position of orthodoxy on these issues

   C. *Aaron's Rod Blossoming*

      i. Most important book on the Church-State relationship

      ii. Written to combat the error of Erastianism

IX. Conclusion

    A. Congress should make no law respecting the establishment of religion (1st amendment)

    B. Duty of the Church to protect itself against any usurpation by the State

Questions

1. What does Aaron's rod represent?

_____

_____

_____

2. What is Erastianism?

_____

_____

_____

3. What is the Catholic model of Church-State jurisdiction?

_____

_____

_____

4. What is the Reformed view of jurisdiction?

_____

_____

_____

5. What are the jurisdictional symbols of enforcement?

_____

_____

_____

6. What is the issue addressed by George Gillespie at the Westminster Assembly?

_____

_____

_____

7. What does the 1st Amendment represent?

_____

_____

_____

8. What is the duty of the Church in regard to the State's power?

_____

_____

_____

9. What happens if the right jurisdictions are not in place?

_____

_____

_____

10. Is congress allowed to make laws respecting the establishment of religion?

_____

_____

_____

Further Reading

Member of the Westminster Assembly, George Gillespie, wrote the following about the separation of Church and State in his book, *Aaron's Rod Blossoming*:

> *"The Scripture holds forth the civil and ecclesiastical power as most distinct; insomuch that it condemned the spiritualizing of the civil power, as well as the secularizing of the ecclesiastical power; state papacy as well as papal state. Church officers may not take the civil sword, nor judges civil causes, Luke 12:13,14; 22:25; Matthew 24:52; 2 Corinthians 19:4; 2 Timothy 2:4. So Uzzah might not touch the ark; nor Saul offer burnt-offerings; nor Uzziah burn incense. I wish we may not have cause to revive the proverb which was used in Ambrose's time: "the Emperors did more covet the priesthood than the priest did covet the empire." Shall it be a sin to church officers to exercise any act of civil government, and shall it be a sin to church officers to exercise any act of civil government, and shall it be no sin to the civil magistrate to engross the whole and sole power of church government? Are not the two powers formally and specifically distinct?"*

But this did not constitute a separation of God from Government as Gillespie explains:

> *"By the law of God I understand* jus divinum naturale, *that is the moral law or Decalogue, as that binds all nations (whether Christian or infidel), being the law of the Creator as King of Nations. The Magistrate, by his authority may, and in duty ought, to keep his subjects with in the bounds of external obedience to the law and publish the external man with external punishments for external trespasses against the law. From this obligation to the Law, and subjection to corrective power of the magistrate, Christian subjects are no more exempted than heathen subjects, but rather more straightly obliged."* [20]

Definitions

Erastianism: The idea that the state is supreme over the church and ecclesiastical matters.

Church Autonomy: The idea that the church is to be untouched by other forms of Government.

The Papal Revolution: A gradual movement within the Roman Catholic Church in which the Pope was declared to be preeminent over every sphere of Government.

Establishmentarianism: An idea that the Civil Government should establish a State Church.

Writing Assignment

During the early struggle for religious liberty in Virginia, dissenting Baptist and Presbyterian churches were at the forefront of a struggle that led to the disestablishment of the state licensure of churches in Virginia. Prior to that time, churches were required to ask the civil government for permission to exist, which only granted permission to the Anglican established church. As part of that debate, the Hanover Presbytery presented a resolution to the legislature notifying lawmakers that "they ask no ecclesiastical establishments for themselves, neither can they approve them when granted to others, and earnestly entreat... that all laws now in force in [Virginia] which countenance religious denominations be repealed." [21] Later in 1811, President James Madison, having been instrumental in establishing religious liberty in Virginia, vetoed an act to incorporate an Anglican church in the District of Columbia. His reason for vetoing the bill "was that incorporation was a form of licensing by which government gave churches permission to operate. Therefore, incorporation was superfluous; government has no jurisdictional authority to tell churches they can or cannot operate." [22] Based on what you have learned in this lesson, write a 500-word essay on the influence of the work of George Gillespie on America's Founding Fathers. In your discussion include some modern examples of how the state has violated this wall of separation.

Recommendations for Further Study

Aaron's Rod Blossoming, by George Gillespie

Letters of Samuel Rutherford, by Samuel Rutherford

The Gospel Ministry, by Thomas Foxcroft

Law and Revolution, by Harold Berman

Christ's Churches Purely Reformed, by Phillip Benedict

Documentary History of the Struggle for Religious liberty in Virginia, by Charles F. James

Unit Two–Lesson 3
The Jurisdiction of the Family

Introduction

The family is the basic institutional cell of all civilization. Of the three spheres of Government established by God, the family is the only human institution that God established while man still enjoyed the perfection of Eden. From the opening chapters of Genesis, we see the institution of the church and state as developing out of the family. In his commentary on Genesis 5:26, John Calvin points out: "We may readily conclude that Seth was an upright and faithful servant of God... after he begat a son, like himself, and had a rightly constituted family, the face of the Church began distinctly to appear, and the worship of God was set up which might continue to posterity."[23] Similarly, regarding the state, theologian B.M. Palmer wrote, "by the coexistence of many households society at large may be constituted." He continued: "The family may be viewed...as the original society from which the states emerge and the church, and every other association known among men.... Neither State nor Church could exist, but of the material which the family affords."[24] Cotton Mather also drew the same connection, writing, "it is evident that families are the nurseries of all societies…well ordered families naturally produce a good order in other societies."[25] Families, then, are the basic organisms of civilization, the eggs from which all other human institutions hatch, including Church and State."

While both church and state have developed naturally out of the family to be separate and independent spheres of government, the family still maintains its own separate and independent sphere of government. The jurisdiction of the family can be broken down into three areas. These include matters surrounding marriage, children, and the family estate. It is important to look to the family in light of its historical relationship with the church and the civil government, in order to understand how encroachments against the family take place; and, historically, encroachments on the jurisdiction of the family have taken place in one of these three areas.

At the beginning of the 21st century, there is a growing idea that the state has a superior authority over each of these areas and state encroachments on marriage, the birth and upbringing of children, and the family estate have been virtually unbridled. The homes and children belonging to the family jurisdiction are not secure against state searches and seizure. Marriages suffer from an unrelenting divorce rate and a growing movement toward homosexuality. Family estates are taxed to compel statist education on children, and death taxes prevent the multigenerational building of family wealth. The last of the old family estates are being swallowed up by the State, because it is no longer worth the money required to maintain them from generation to generation. Making difficulties worse is the fact that many of the social ethics asserted by our enemies of yesterday are assumed and rigidly defended by our friends today. Feminism, property taxes, compulsory education, birth control, no fault divorce, and egalitarianism in the workplace are all realities assumed and defended by a majority in the Christian church.

The Christian statesman must recognize that the battle for the family is crucial to the battle for civilization. Socialist Bolshevik Aleksandra Kollontai commented, "The capitalists themselves are not aware of the fact that the family of old…is the best weapon to stifle the proletarian [communist] effort. . .".[26] Similarly, in his popular history Modern Times, Paul Johnson wrote, "The real antithesis to National Socialism was individualism, a society where private arrangements took priority over public, where the family was the favored social unit and where the voluntary unit was paramount. . . . A society in which the family, as opposed to the political party and the ideological programme, was the starting point for reconstruction, was the answer to the totalitarian evil."[27] The family, not the civil government, is the greatest institutional safeguard of liberty, and the Christian family is the most powerful weapon against statism and tyranny.

In this lecture, President of Heritage Defense, Don Hart, will focus in on the current state of parental rights in the United States. He will discuss how various State agencies have been formed which brake down the family and assume jurisdiction over children. In the end, he will demonstrate the important role of the Christian statesman in restoring the family back to its proper jurisdiction.

Lecture Outline

1. Introduction by Doug Phillips

2. Herman Humphrey (New England 1840)

3. 4th Amendment of the Constitution

    A. The right of the people to be secure in their persons, houses, papers, and effects

4. Texas Constitution, Article 1, Section 9

    A. The people shall be secure in their persons, houses, papers and possessions, from all unreasonable seizures or searches

5. Texas Family Code, Section 222.003

    A. A person who takes possession of a child without a court order is immune from civil liability if, at the time possession is taken, there is reasonable cause to believe there is an immediate danger to the physical health or safety of the child.

6. Texas Family Code, Section 262.104, Section 262.106, Section 262.101, Section 262.201

7. 1983-1990-California: McMartin Preschool Abuse Trial

    A. The longest and most expensive criminal trial in American history

    B. Methodology used in this case

    C. Absurd allegations

    D. Vulnerability of children

8. Research on Children's Susceptibility

    A. Interviewer's bias

    B. Leading questions and suggestive techniques

C. Clarke-Stewart study 1989

D. The effect of peer-pressure on a child

E. The effects of being interviewed by someone with high status

9. Texas Polygamy Case 2008 (FLDS)

A. Questionable source

B. Questionable timing

C. Questionable allegation

D. Guilt by association

10. CPS Activity Described as a Civil Activity, Not a Criminal One

11. Parents Have to Be Diligent in Changing Some of These Laws

Questions

1. Should the State have an interest in protecting children?

_____

_____

_____

2. Should Protective Services continue to exist?

_____

_____

_____

3. Who has the jurisdiction over non-criminal cases in the family?

_____

_____

_____

4. What is the summation of the fourth Amendment of the Constitution?

_____

_____

_____

5. What is one of the biggest problems with the McMartin Preschool Abuse Trial?

_____

_____

_____

6. What is one of the researches done on children's susceptibility?

_____

_____

_____

7. What is the exclusionary rule?

_____

_____

_____

8. How is Social Services exempt from the exclusionary rule?

_____

_____

_____

9. Should Social Services workers be allowed in the home without a warrant?

_____

_____

_____

10. How were children manipulated in the McMartin case?

_____

_____

_____

Further Reading

In his book, *The Family*, B.M. Palmer writes concerning the family, headship, and the nature of authority:

> *"It was a sublime exercise of wisdom and power when God created the heavens and the earth, impressing upon matter its various properties, and determining the methods by which its imprisoned forces should be developed, But this was as nothing compared with the difficulties which emerge when He created a living soul, made in His own image, endowed with reason, personality and will. Whether we contemplate it in the history of angels or of men, it was a mighty event when a being was fashioned with intelligence and will separate from that of the Creator, moving upon its own plane, under the guidance of his own thought, and under the promptings of his own choice. "What shall be the relation of this wall to the will that is higher? And how shall the subordination be maintained, consistently with the spontaneity and freedom of that which is controlled. These are questions upon which are hinged all the problems of Providence and of Grace; and they have their outworking in the continuous history of both.*
>
> *Angels, who steadfastly held to the allegiance which they owed to Jehovah, and angels who, in the exercise of the same freedom, fell from their loyalty and became apostate, both declare the nature and peril of the problem of separate wills, which must, somehow or other, be coordinated. Man, too, under temptation, fails in the exercise of his personal freedom; and the great mystery of Grace is, how to recover*

that enslaved and depraved will, and to bring it again into harmony with the will of the Supreme, without contravening the spontaneity of its own determinations. The reader need not be told that we are plunged just here into the entire mystery of the Spirit's work in regeneration and sanctification, in which we are "made willing in the day of His power."

Now, it is exactly this problem that is brought down into the sphere of the Family; where the first stones in the social structure are laid, and the foundation of all government and law is placed, in the subordination of concurrent wills. There is the will of the husband and wife, the joint rulers over the domestic state and there is the will of parent and child, in the union of obedience with authority. The great problem of God's sovereign control over the spontaneous will of the creature finds its best illustration within the government of the Family; and we can partly see how power blends with freedom, as the factors of a common product."

Definitions

Exclusionary Rule: A rule of evidence which states that evidence illegally seized by law enforcement officers in violation of a suspect's right to be free from unreasonable searches and seizures cannot be used against the suspect in a criminal prosecution.

Writing Assignment

The sociologist Carl Zimmerman pointed out that the decline of each of the old world empires correlated with the decline of the family. There were four historical attributes of the collapse of the family, which in turn led to the collapse of the state.

First, there was an almost universal corruption and disregard for the marriage agreement. Divorce was unbridled and a large segment of the population shifted toward homosexuality. Second, the nation experienced a decreasing birthrate. Abortion, exposure, and the use of birth control were pervasive. Fewer children were born and those children that were born were seen as belonging to the State. Third, there was a denigration of the authority and role of parents. Parental rights and duties with regard to the upbringing of children were broken down. Rebellious claims of independence asserted by children against their parents were accepted as normative. Finally, there was a drastic rise in juvenile and adult delinquency. The culture became amoral and the activities of parents and their children alike were no longer focused on the felicity of the family estate. The family relationship became merely an emotional bond, and the home, merely a place for the cohabitation of individuals. As the family died, the state died with it. In at least 500 words, describe the state of the modern family in relation to these warning signs. Discuss how some of these influences might be changed if a biblical framework for the family and culture were adopted.

Recommendations for Further Study

The Family, by B. M. Palmer

The Family and Civilization, by Carl Zimmerman

From Cottage to Workstation, by Alan C. Carlson

The Puritan Family, by Edmund S. Morgan

Family Reformation, by Scott Brown

Unit Three

Unit Three–Lesson 1
Biblical Faith and the United States Constitution

Introduction

Tremendous effort has gone into popularizing the idea that America is a nation of religious pluralism and that the federal constitution was intended to be a wholly "secular" and "non-religious" document. Modern scholars have worked tirelessly to excommunicate the founding fathers from the church post-mortem, alleging that they were deist; this even though deist made up less than one percent of the population during America's founding era. However, the impact of Christianity on the United States Constitution, on the founding fathers, and on those who argued for the ratification of the federal constitution is undeniable by any honest scholar. Yet, the more important issue of faith in relation to the United States Constitution is not merely whether the American founders were Christian; without a doubt they were. The most important issue relating to the constitution is how faithful their descendants will be to their legacy of Christian statesmanship. Constitutional scholar, James McClellan explained:

"For it has been said that every country possesses two distinct constitutions that exist side by side. One of these is the formal written constitution of modern times; the other is the old 'unwritten' one of political conventions, habits, and ways of living together in the civil social order that have developed among many people over the centuries. . . . So it is possible to speak of a 'visible' and an 'invisible' constitution." [28]

For instance, the first question of the Westminster catechism was written to teach that the highest purpose of each and every man is to glorify God and to enjoy Him forever. If the Christian is to take such a faith seriously, then our political conventions, habits, social norms, and every other aspect of our social order must be made to serve that end.

The Constitution may be read, but it cannot be properly interpreted without a firm foundation of biblical faith. Much of the debate over how the constitution should be interpreted has been between two primary schools of thought. The progressive school of thought asserts that the constitution is a living document and must be interpreted in light of modern changing social norms. The strict constructionist school of thought asserts that the constitution is a fixed written document and must be interpreted on the basis of what the original founding fathers intended. It is important to realize that these views are interchanged between the types of men that John Adams warned against. Progressives typically are bewildered by the idea of a fixed constitution that is at odds with those who desire to exercise "passions unbridled by morality and religion." Yet, on the other hand, it must be understood that the constitution is not an infallible document written by infallible men. Adams warned that the constitution is practically powerless unless there is a nation of morally upright people to properly interpret and apply it. Constitutional concepts such as liberty, law, order, or justice cannot be properly interpreted or applied without reference to Scripture. Instead, the Christian faith must be the very basis for progress and security of a nation.

In this lecture, Constitutional lawyer Doug Phillips will reveal why being rooted in biblical morality is essential to a proper understanding of law and liberty. America's founders were not men who placed their faith aside in matters of public importance. In like manner, the Constitution they drafted cannot be properly interpreted apart from an understanding and appreciation of the Christian principles they championed. Likewise, the Christian statesman cannot set his Christian faith aside in matters of politics and social significance. Instead, the glorification and enjoyment of God must be the starting point and the end of all of social interaction.

Lecture Outline

1. Establish a Christian Worldview

    A. God's Law must be supreme

    B. The importance of biblical ethics

    C. There is no neutrality

2. Impediments to Christian Discernment

    A. Emotionalism

    B. Semi-rationalism

3. Biblical Foundations for Answering Ethical Issues

    A. The Puritan example

    B. Richard Baxter: *Practical Discourses*

4. A Crisis of Methodology

    A. Ethical relativism: humanistic philosophy

        i. Situational Ethics

        ii. Majoritarian Ethics

        iii. Pragmatism

    B. The Attack on the Sufficiency of Scripture

        i. Applicability of the Old Testament

        ii. Confusion on Christian liberty

        iii. Orthopraxy is legalism

5. The Need for Christian Apologetics

    A. The example of Jesus

    B. Example of Paul

6. Biblical and Humanistic Legal Advocacy

    A. The unbiblical nature of modern philosophy and legal advocacy

    B. The biblical doctrine of legal advocacy is to promote God's righteous order and to seek God's righteous justice for the client

7. Issues Facing 21st Century Lawyers

A. Loss of national identity

B. The rising global community

C. Departure from the Law of God

D. Usurpation of family and church jurisdictions

E. Marginalization in the Christian community

F. Pacification of men through sexuality, sports, entertainment, and technology

8. Incrementalism

A. Incrementalism may not involve a fundamental compromise

B. Incrementalism may not foreclose the possibility of future success

Questions

1. Why are ethical considerations important?

_____

_____

_____

2. What do we mean that our orthopraxy should line up with our orthodoxy?

_____

_____

_____

3. What is the conclusion to Semi-Rationalism?

_____

_____

_____

4. What are we to look for when searching the Scriptures to find answers for ethical considerations?

_____

_____

_____

5. What has God given us for all matters of law, ethics, and public policy?

_____

_____

_____

6. What is it meant by the word *apologia*?

_____

_____

_____

7. What is the first duty of a lawyer?

_____

_____

_____

8. What are some issues facing 21st century lawyers?

_____

_____

_____

9. Is God concerned only about spiritual things?

_____

_____

_____

10. What is wrong with pragmatism?

_____

_____

_____

Further Reading

In his *Bonifacius*, Cotton Mather wrote on the importance of Christians in society to do good. According to Mather, since unbelievers through depravity are incapable of any real good that is glorifying to God, it is incumbent on Christians to glorify God by serving the local communities in which they live:

> "It is to be feared, that we too seldom enquire after our opportunities to do good. Our opportunities to do good are our talents. An awful account must be rendered unto the Great God, concerning our use of the talents, wherewith he has entrusted us, in these precious opportunities. We do not use our opportunities, many times because we do not know what they are; and many times, the reason why we do not know, is because we do not think. Our opportunities to do good, lay by un-regarded, and un-improved; and so 'tis but a mean account that can be given of them. We read of a thing, which we deride as often as we behold; there is, that makes himself poor, and yet has great riches. It is a good thing too frequently exemplified, in our opportunities to do good, which are some of our most valuable riches. Many a man seems to reckon himself destitute of those talents; as if there were nothing for him to do: He pretends he is not in a condition to do any good. Alas! Poor man; what can he do? My friend, think again; think often. Enquire what your opportunities are. You will doubtless find them to be more than you were aware of. Plain men dwelling in tents, persons of a very ordinary character, may in a way of bright piety, prove persons of extraordinary usefulness . . . .

This then is the next proposal. Without abridging yourselves of your occasional thoughts on the question, often every day, what good may I do? State a time now and then for more deliberate thoughts upon it. Can't you find a time, (suppose, once a week, yea, and how agreeably, on the Lord's Day,) to take that question into your consideration; what is there that I may do for the service of the glorious lord, and for the welfare of those for whom you ought to be concerned?" [29]

Definitions

Ethics: The discipline of dealing with what is good and bad and with moral duty and obligation.

Apologetics: The vindication of the Christian philosophy of life against all other philosophies of life.

Pragmatism: A philosophical approach that seeks to evaluate ethics solely in terms of the expected success of its practical application without regard to the morality of the application itself.

Rationalism: A philosophical theory that deems human reason to be the foundation of certainty in matters of ascertaining truth.

Gnosticism: An ancient heresy that held that material things are intrinsically secular, and that spiritual things are sacred and holy

Writing Assignment

In 1797, writing to the Massachusetts Militia, John Adams wrote:

"We have no government armed with power capable of contending with human passions unbridled by morality and religion. . . . Our Constitution was made only for a religious and moral people. It is wholly inadequate for the government of any other."

For Adams, the faith of the nation was more vital to the nation's security and order than a well-drafted federal constitution. Using what you have learned in this lesson, write at least 500 words about why John Adams would have relied so heavily on the Christian faith and public morality as a safeguard to the Constitution.

Recommendations for Further Study

Institute on the Constitution, by John Eidsmoe

Liberty, Order, and Justice, by James McClellan

The General Principles of Constitutional Law, by Thomas Cooley

Commentaries on the United States Constitution, by Joseph Story

The Roots of Liberty, Editor, Ellis Sandoz

Unit Three–Lesson 2
Biblical Faith and Social Ethics

Introduction

Jesus Christ is the ruler of the Nations. America's founding fathers were very conscious of this fact, understanding that to ignore the precepts of Christ in matter of public policy was to invite the judgment of God on a nation. The judgment of God is an idea that has been virtually ignored in our modern culture, even among some Christians. When calamitous events occur that cripple a nation's population, infrastructure, economy, or morale, it is an extremely unpopular thing to mention that such events might indicate the displeasure and judgment of God. For the evolutionist and secular humanists, we live in an universe governed, not by God, but by time and chance. Therefore, when calamitous things occur it is said to be a matter of tragic circumstances caused by chance.

The idea that civil governments fall under national judgment for failing to honor the sovereign authority of God in the civil sphere is not only a reoccurring theme in Scripture, but is also a reoccurring theme throughout history. In his magnum opus, *The City of God*, Bishop Aurelius Augustine of Hippo, discussed the destruction of Rome, at that time a Christian nation. One of the most interesting sections is presented as Augustine confronted the question of, why do the righteous also suffer in national judgment. Augustine's answer was a different one than perhaps many leaders in the church might give today. Augustine held that the nation was evil and that evil was not restrained because Christians had failed in their duty to be salt and light in their communities. Christians had become so attached to this world and their lives in it, that they feared to resist evil lest they lose the praise of men, public respectability, and be seen as foolish.

Hence, the Christian statesman, though he never runs for office, never writes legislations, or never argues a case before the Supreme Court, if he acts with integrity in his local community, by evangelizing, carrying out acts of Christian charity, rebuking public wrongs, and praying with diligence, is more powerful in leading a nation to God then a thousand politicians who for fear of losing respectability among carefully tailored political coalitions never fail to resist evil or win the hearts and minds of their community for Christ in any meaningful fashion.

A comparison of these two types of Christian statesmen might be best illustrated by the destruction of Sodom and Gomorrah in Genesis chapters 18 and 19. Even though Abraham was not even a citizen of Sodom or Gomorrah, he prayed that God would stray His judgment to the point that God would have spared Sodom and Gomorrah if five righteous men were found there. When the angels arrived in the city to seek out those men, Lot saw the angels arrive while he was siting in the gate. Some have understood that Lot was carrying out some civil function since the gate of an ancient city was a place where civil duties were performed. In the end, Lot had moved toward Sodom for his own prosperity's sake; and though Lot had lived in the city for some time and had sat in the gate, he had failed to capture the hearts and minds of even five men for the glory of God. In Genesis 19:29, we find that Lot only escaped the judgment that came on the city, not for his own righteousness, but because God remembered Abraham. So who had been the better statesman: Lot, an affluent citizen who obtained a civil position to effect change, or Abraham, who was not even a citizen of the cities, but who faithfully interceded on behalf of the city.

Christians may forfeit a respectful position of power, and economic security by being a faithful testimony to the community around them. Yet, the Christian statesman who is diligent in being salt and light in his local communities are particularly important to the prosperity, longevity, and public welfare of a nation. In this lecture, Doug Phillips will lead a discussion about the various ethical questions in which Christians cannot ignore the culture around them, but must be salt and light. He will elaborate on the manner in which Christian faith is vital to our public welfare.

Lecture Outline

1. Are People More than Their Genes?

2. All Ethical Questions Should be Answered by Christians

3. Humans and Animals Don't have the Same Standard of Ethics

4. Two Types of Arguments

    A. Hermeneutic, exegetical argument

    B. Broad, sweeping argument

5. Three things in Scripture that Represent a Nation in Judgment

    A. Murder of the innocent

    B. Immorality and perversion

    C. Feminism

6. Genesis 9

    A. Government and capital punishment are introduced in the same time

    B. Three reason the Bible allows killing:

        1. Defense of Self and Others

        2. Justifiable warfare

        3. Execution for Capital Crimes

7. Defense of Innocent Life is the First Principal of Government

8. Christian Must Love Life

9. Biblical Philosophy of Education

    A. Education is inescapable religious discipline

    B. Government schools are wrong because they exist

    C. The importance of maintaining our independence from the government

10. Discussions on Different Case Scenarios

11. The Role of Money in the Kingdom of God

12. Embryonic Stem Cell Research

13. The Concept of Christian Burial

A. Cremation viewed as pagan until the 20th century

B. Biblical pattern: burial, preservation, the resurrection of the death

C. Pagan nation believed in burning the body

14. Thoughts on Ethical issues

A. Distinctions between organ donation and organ harvesting

B. Organ harvesting is a crime

C. Differences between autopsy and fetal stem cell donation

D. Fetal stem cell donations maliciously driven by politics

15. The Importance of Fighting for the Premises

16. Discussions on Different Scenarios

17. Conclusions

A. We do not have the liberty to take the life of one person to save another

B. We should be pro-life with no exception

C. The importance of humility before the Lord

D. The danger of our conscious being seared

Questions

1. Are there any ethical questions that Christians should not try to answer?

_____

_____

_____

2. Should someone that does not believe in protecting innocent life be considered for public office?

_____

_____

_____

3. Why are public schools wrong?

_____

_____

_____

4. What are some of the types of arguments used when looking at ethical and bioethical arguments?

_____

_____

_____

5. What are the three reasons when killing is allowed in the Bible?

_____

_____

_____

6. What is the first duty of Government?

_____

_____

_____

7. Why was cremation viewed as pagan up to the 20th century?

_____

_____

_____

8. What is the difference between organ donation and organ harvesting?

_____

_____

_____

9. What is the difference between autopsy and fetal stem cell donation?

_____

_____

_____

10. Should we ever take the life of one to save another?

_____

_____

_____

Further Reading

In *The City of God*, Aurelius Augustine, gives an answer to questions regarding why many righteous citizens of Rome suffered along with the wicked when the city was sacked:

> *"First of all, they must humbly consider those very sins which have provoked God to fill the world with such terrible disasters;. . . . Though he do not fall into gross enormity of wickedness, and abandoned viciousness, and abominable profanity, yet he slips into some sins, either rarely or so much the more frequently as the sins seem of less*

account. . . . For often we wickedly blind ourselves to the occasions of teaching and admonishing them, sometimes even of reprimanding and chiding them, either because we shrink from the labor or are ashamed to offend them, or because we fear to lose good friendships, lest this should stand in the way of our advancement, or injure us in some worldly matter, which either our covetous disposition desires to obtain, or our weakness shrinks from losing. So that, although the conduct of wicked men is distasteful to the good, and therefore they do not fall with them into that damnation which in the next life awaits such persons, yet, because they spare their damnable sins through fear, therefore, even though their own sins be slight and venial, they are justly scourged with the wicked in this world, though in eternity they quite escape punishment. . . .

They abstain from interference, because they fear that, if it fail of good effect, their own safety or reputation may be damaged or destroyed; not because they see that their preservation and good name are needful, that they may be able to influence those who need their instruction, but rather because they weakly relish the flattery and respect of men, and fear the judgments of the people, and the pain or death of the body; that is to say, their non-intervention is the result of selfishness, and not of love. Accordingly this seems to me to be one principal reason why the good are chastised along with the wicked, when God is pleased to visit with temporal punishments the profligate manners of a community.... These selfish persons have more cause to fear than those to whom it was said through the prophet, "He is taken away in his iniquity, but his blood will I require at the watchman's hand."

For watchmen or overseers of the people are appointed in churches, that they may unsparingly rebuke sin. Nor is that man guiltless of the sin we speak of, who, though he be not a watchman, yet sees in the conduct of those with whom the relationships of this life bring him into contact, many things that should be blamed, and yet overlooks them, fearing to give offence, and lose such worldly blessings as may legitimately be desired, but which he too eagerly grasps. Then, lastly, there is another reason why the good are afflicted with temporal calamities—the reason which Job's case exemplifies: that the human spirit may be proved, and that it may be manifested with what fortitude of pious trust, and with how unmercenary a love, it cleaves to God."

Definitions

Exegesis: The discipline of drawing the meaning out of a text without reference to external considerations.

Hermeneutics: The science and discipline of interpreting the Scriptures

Bioethics: The study of ethics related to medical and biological research and practice.

Writing Assignment

After the end of World War II the west discovered the brutal and unspeakable atrocities committed by the Germans in the name of science. Some have said that science has become the predominant religion of the age. A major modern criticism of Christianity is that it forces its morality on a host of areas of scientific research and practice such as stem cell research, cloning, and abortion. At the root of this criticism is a belief that science is somehow transcendent to moral considerations. Using what you have learned in this lesson choose a topic discussed in the lecture and write at least 500 words about why the Scripture must be advanced as a legitimate restarting force on the sciences.

Recommendations for Further Study

The Divine Challenge, by John Byl

The Biblical Basis for Modern Science, by John Morris

The City of God, by Aurelius Augustine

Calvinism in History, by Nathaniel McFetridge

Ultimate Questions, by John Blanchard

Unit Three–Lesson 3
Resistance to Tyranny, Obedience to God

Introduction

What are Christians to do when their rulers are tyrannical? Since the beginning of the Reformation, the tyranny of civil rulers had forced men such as Martin Luther, John Calvin, Christopher Goodman, Theodore Beza, John Knox, George Buchanan and several others to search the Scriptures to find answers for questions such as: (1) What is the nature and extent of the authority of a civil magistrate?; (2) When is it lawful to resist a civil authority by force?; and (3) When is it lawful to disobey a law issued by a lawful magistrate? While these men differed in some respects, they developed a striking consensus, which eventually led to the greatest collapse of tyranny and widespread reign of liberty that the world had seen since the fall of Rome and the rise of Christendom.

Five core doctrines were systematically developed and propagated by the Calvinistic reformers, all of which substantially limited the authority of the civil magistrate. These were: (1) the absolute sovereignty of God over the civil magistrate; (2) the recognition of a civil covenant as the basis for social order; (3)

a constitutional standard of higher law; (4) the right and duty to resist tyrants and; (5) the duty of private individuals to practice civil disobedience when the laws of man come into conflict with the laws of God. This central focus on the transcendence of God over every aspect of the civil realm, combined with man's duty to bring the whole of his mind and conduct into conformity to God's divine prerogatives, is ultimately what separates the Calvinist resistance theory from the lawless rebellion of the Anabaptists and the bloody revolutions of the Rationalists "[O]n the one hand, fanatic and barbarous men are furiously endeavoring to overturn the order established by God," warned Calvin, "and, on the other, the flatterers of princes, extolling their power without measure, hesitate not to oppose it to the government of God. Unless we meet both extremes, the purity of the faith will perish." [30]

For this reason the doctrine of interposition was expounded which guarded against both the tyranny of the civil magistrate as well as guards against the lawlessness of the masses. The doctrine of interposition holds that a tyrant in a legitimate place of authority can only be resisted by another who also sits in a legitimate place of authority, even if the resisting magistrate sits in a lower seat of authority. The doctrine of interposition is based on the firm persuasion that God is sovereign and that the obligation of civil government is to carry out His divine prerogatives for the citizens of the state. A lower magistrate has a higher duty to God, the social covenant, and the national constitution, and therefore the lower magistrate has not only the right, but also a duty to resist tyranny.

This doctrine of interposition was adopted as the basis of the American war against English aggression. King George of England had failed to protect the American colonies against the unlawful aggression from the Parliament of England. While the King of England held a legitimate place of authority over all of the colonies, the British Parliament had no legitimate authority to govern the colonies. From the beginning, the colonies were governed by their own representative governments. It is important to understand that the names written down by the signers to the Declaration of Independence did not have weight to sign on their own authority. Instead, these men signed as representatives of the various colonial congresses who were in a lawful position of authority to resist the tyranny of the King of England.

The doctrine of interposition was built into the Federal Constitution itself as civil power was divided into branches of government; and the states, also having republican forms of government, reserved a superior authority over the federal government. This constitutional division of power, the constitutional checks and balances, and federalism were all intended to prevent a tyranny from coming to power, and to provide the maximum framework for other magistrates and branches of government to practice interposing if they ever had need. In addition, the framers of the Constitution included the Second Amendment in the Bill of Rights. This ensured that the people would have the right to bear arms and to maintain a military, as well as the means to resist tyranny by military force.

In this lecture, Larry Pratt will discuss the history, the nature, and the importance of the Second Amendment right to bear arms. He will explain the ways in which modern political forces have attempted to erode this constitutional right and what the Christian statesman can do to preserve these rights.

Lecture Outline

The Importance of the Second Amendment

1. The Historical Background of the Second Amendment

A. The Second Amendment is rooted in the Common Laws of England

B. Many founders were the grandchildren of refugees of the English Civil War

C. William Blackstone

2. The Purpose for a Well-Regulated Militia

A. The English Civil war settled the debate concerning who controlled the militia

B. William Blackstone also upheld the Militia as a legitimate institution

C. George Mason defined the Militia as every able man excepting elected officials

3. The Militia Act of 1792

A. Required militarily able men to have a rifle, ammunition, and keep it at home

B. The National Guard is not a true militia

4. Is the Right to Bear Arms a Collective Right?

A. The Second Amendment to the Constitution gives the right for individual people and not for States

B. Constitution gives Congress basic jurisdiction over the Militia, not the States

5. The Interpretation of the United States Constitution

    A. The Constitution must be read literally according to its original intent

6. Christianity and Gun Ownership

    A. Self defense and the defense of family is required by Scripture

    B. Exodus 22

    C. Proverbs 25:26

7. The Role of Government

    A. Romans 13 requires the civil magistrate to be a terror to evildoers

    B. The role of government is not preemptive

8. Prohibition on Guns

    A. Most attempts to keep guns out of the hands of criminals take the form of a prohibition on law-abiding citizens

9. Current Issues

    A. The Gun Show Loophole

    B. Gun Registration

    C. The Unconstitutional Brady Law

    D. The Gun Lock Controversy

    E. Gun-Free Zones

10. Constitutional Violations Connected with Gun Rights

    A. Campaign Finance

        i. An attack on free speech

        ii. Freedom of press an individual right

    B. Search and Seizure

    C. Environmental Extremism

    D. The United Nations

11. Principles of Confrontational Politics

Questions

1. In Common Law, who was responsible for the public defense?

    _____

    _____

    _____

2. According to William Blackstone, what is the purpose of a militia?

    _____

    _____

    _____

3. What was English Enlightenment philosopher Jeremy Bentham's program for restoring the peace?

    _____

    _____

    _____

4. When and where did America's first full time police force appear?

    _____

    _____

    _____

5. What is the gun show "loophole"?

    _____

    _____

    _____

6.   Registration has been required in Canada since 1934.

_____

_____

_____

7.   How has campaign finance reform lead to a violation of the right to freedom of speech?

_____

_____

_____

8.   How does the United Nations pose a threat to our right to bear arms?

_____

_____

_____

9.   How does the Scripture teach us to petition the government?

_____

_____

_____

10. What type of arms do citizens have the constitutional right to own?

_____

_____

_____

Further Reading

The following is a selection from the *Magna Charta*, one of the greatest ancient constitutions of the Common Law and an antecedent to the United States Constitution. In this selection, the Charter establishes a constitutional right to take up arms against tyrants:

"Moreover, all these aforesaid customs and liberties, the observances of which we have granted in our kingdom as far as pertains to us towards our men, shall be observed in all of our kingdom, as well clergy as laymen, as far as pertains to them towards their men.

Since, moreover, for God and the amendment of our kingdom and for the better allaying of the quarrel that has arisen between us and our barons, we have granted all these concessions, desirous that they should enjoy them in complete and firm endurance forever, we give and grant to them the underwritten security, namely, that the barons choose five and twenty barons of the kingdom, whomsoever they will, who shall be bound with all their might, to observe and hold, and cause to be observed, the peace and liberties we have granted and confirmed to them by this our present Charter, so that if we, or our justiciar, or our bailiffs or any one of our officers, shall in anything be at fault towards anyone, or shall have broken any one of the articles of this peace or of this security, and the offense be notified to four barons of the aforesaid five and twenty, the said four barons shall repair to us (or our justiciar, if we are out of the realm) and, laying the transgression before us, petition to have that transgression redressed without delay. And if we shall not have corrected the transgression (or, in the event of our being out of the realm, if our justiciar shall not have corrected it) within forty days, reckoning from the time it has been intimated to us (or to our justiciar, if we should be out refer that matter to the rest of the five and twenty barons, and those five and twenty barons shall, together with the community of the whole realm, distrain? and distress us in all possible ways, namely, by seizing our castles, lands, possessions, and in any other way they can, until redress has been obtained as they deem fit, saving harming our own person, and the persons of our queen and children; and when redress has been obtained, they shall resume their old relations towards us. And let whoever in the country desires it, swear to obey the orders of the said five and twenty barons for the execution of all the aforesaid matters, and along with them, to molest us to the utmost of his power; and we publicly and freely grant leave to everyone who wishes to swear, and we shall never forbid anyone to swear.... And we shall procure nothing from anyone, directly or indirectly, whereby any part of these concessions and liberties might be revoked or diminished; and if any such things have been procured, let it be void and null, and we shall never use it personally or by another. ...

Wherefore we will and firmly order that the English Church be free, and that the men in our kingdom have and hold all the aforesaid liberties, rights, and concessions, well and peaceably, freely and quietly, fully and wholly, for themselves and their heirs, of us and our heirs, in all respects and in all places forever, as is aforesaid. An oath, moreover, has been taken, as well on our part as on the art of the barons, that all these conditions aforesaid shall be kept in good faith and without evil intent."

Definitions

Calvinistic Resistance Theory: A biblical doctrine which holds that a civil magistrate must be obeyed as an authority established by God, but in the event of tyranny he may be resisted by a lawful lower magistrate.

Militia: A military force that is raised from the citizen population to supplement and sometimes to oppose the regular army in an emergency.

Tyranny: The exertion of power by an authority into an area over which he has no lawful authority.

Writing Assignment

While in England John Adams visited the site of one of Cromwell's victories over Charles I. John Adams grew indignant when he realized that the English knew nothing of the history. He wrote:

"I was provoked and asked 'and do Englishmen so soon forget the ground where liberty was fought for?' Tell your neighbors and your children that this is holy ground; much holier than that on which your churches stand. All England should come in a pilgrimage to this hill once a year."

John Adams obviously had great respect for the historical figures that had impressed on him the importance to resist tyranny. Write an essay of at least 500 words about how we might also pay respects to those who fought for liberty against tyranny in this nation.

Recommendations for Further Study

The Second Amendment, by David Barton

Vindiciae Contra Tyrannos, by Stephanus Janus Brutus

The Founders' Second Amendment, by Stephen Halbrook

Confrontational Politics, by Sen. H.L. Richardson, Ret

Unit Three–Lesson 4
Biblical Economics

Introduction

Economics is perhaps one of the most important subjects for the Christian Statesman to study and understand, because money and economics affect nearly every aspect of both our public and private lives. Every economic system is centered on a bargain and exchange in which parties come to the market to bargain and exchange one item of value for another item of value. In an ethical marketplace, parties are free to bargain for value, but there must be no fraud or deceit in the exchange. In Proverbs we learn that "a false balance is abomination to the LORD: but a just weight is His delight."[31] A scale is uneven when the value of a bargain for exchange is fraudulent or deceptive.

The Bible speaks in depth about money and economics both as it relates to the private individual and the civil government. America's founders understood the biblical and historical precedents set for economics. They built a constitutional system of money that would protect the national economy from instability, while at the same time provide a system with the potential for tremendous growth in the world market. However, as greed, covetousness, and materialism grew among civil powers and the banking system, the American monetary system was turned on its head. If the Christian Statesman is to understand the nature of the financial markets, the monetary system, the banking system, and why world nations are inevitably prone to economic crisis and even collapse, he must look to the Scripture and then examine the modern deviations from that precedent.

At the core of Biblical Economics is the eighth commandment; thou shall not steal. An important derivative of this commandment, as it relates to the monetary system is found in Leviticus 19:35-37; God commands, "Do not use dishonest standards when measuring length, weight or quantity. Use honest scales and honest weights, an honest ephah and an honest hin." This means that the value of exchange should be measurable and there should be no dishonesty or fraud regarding the true value of actual money or goods being exchanged. If a trades man was to tip the scale to receive more money than had actually been bargained for, it is a form of stealing. Moreover, to represent a gold coin in an exchange for goods, as authentic and valued at its full weight while knowing the coin is only gold plated is a form of theft.

This principle would seem easy enough to understand for most. Yet, virtually every modern nation has established a monetary system based on unjust scales, which allows for banks to rob the public of their wealth. Hence, the relationship between America's civil rulers and the Federal Reserve Bank is aptly described in Isaiah 1:23, "Your rulers are rebels, partners with thieves; they all love bribes and chase after gifts. They do not defend the cause of the fatherless; the widow's case does not come before them." Paper money and coins issued by modern nations and banks are representatives of unbalanced scales since they are worth far less than the value ascribed to them in the market place.

In this lecture, attorney and legal historian, Dr. Edwin Vieia Jr. will provide a brief history of the United States dollar. He will speak about how our founding fathers intended America to have a monetary system that was based on gold and silver. In fact, the Constitution required that the States use nothing else. Dr. Vieia will reveal what went wrong and how greed and political corruption subverted the entire framework of the monetary system and established a system which is the fertilizer for economic crisis. Finally, he will uncover the importance of an ethical standard of economics and explain why the study of economics is essential to every Christian statesman.

Lecture Outline

1. Introduction

A. In 1983 the first edition of *Pieces of Eight* was published.

2. The Basics of Constitutional Money

A. The subject of Constitutional Money is quite simple

B. Money is only mentioned a few times in the United States Constitution

3. What is a Dollar?

A. Paper cannot be money anymore than paper can be a cow

B. The dollar originated in Spain and perhaps earlier in Austria

C. The dollar was later mentioned in Article 1 section 9 of the United States Constitution.

D. The Bill of Rights also requires a jury for matters of 20 dollars or more.

4. The Adoption of the Dollar by the United States

A. Thomas Jefferson was the father of the United States Monetary System

B. Value of the dollar was set at the average weight of the coinage

C. The Coinage Act of 1792 defined the constitutional dollar as: "of the value of the Spanish mill dollar as the same as now current and to contain 371.25 grains of pure silver."

5. The Constitutional Dollar

A. Article 1 section 9 of the United States Constitution.

   i. No State shall coin money

   ii. No State shall issue bills of credit

   iii. No State shall make anything but gold or silver coin a tender in payment of debts

B. Article 1 Section 8

   i. Congress shall have the power to coin money regulating the value thereof, and of foreign coin

   ii. William Blackstone defined regulating money as "setting the amount of Gold or Silver in some subsidiary coin at the right arithmetical ratio with the standard"

6. The Introduction of Unconstitutional Paper Money

A. In 1862, the Union Congress passed the Legal Tender Act allowing for the federal issuance of bills of credit.

B. There is no constitutional authority granted to the Federal Congress to issue bills of credit

C. The Supreme Court upheld the issuance of bills of credit

D. The States made the bills of credit legal tender although the Constitution only allowed States to make gold legal tender

7. Fractional Reserve Banking

A. Fractional Reserve Banking is a means to redistribute wealth through the issuance of bills of credit in excess of the actual standard of the gold and silver deposited.

B. The National Banking Acts of 1863 and 1864, created a system of national banks that were empowered to generate bank issued paper currency on the basis of the value of government debt

8. The Federal Reserve Act of 1913

A. The Federal Reserve Act brought all banks under the authority of the Federal Reserve Board

B. The Act was intended to stabilize the threats of depression inherent in the fractional reserve banking system

C. A national depression struck in 1921

D. The bank collapsed in 1932

9. The End of the Gold Standard

A. Gold was seized under Franklin D. Roosevelt to save the banks from the obligation to pay the promised debt on demand

B. Banks were also given the privilege of refusing to pay their promised debts to depositors for six or eight months out of the year

C. There has not been a Supreme Court challenge of the constitutionality of the American monetary system since Roosevelt's Reforms

D. This put a final end to the Constitutional Gold Standard as the basis for our national monetary system

10. The End of the Dollar

A. In 1968, Congress ordered the Treasury to no longer exchange Federal Reserve notes for silver coinage

B. After 1968 money became fiat having no real value for exchange

11. The Roosevelt Reforms and the Commerce Clause

A. The National Industrial Recovery Act organized all of the industries in the United States into industrial cartels at which the President was the head

B. The Supreme Court ruled many of Roosevelt's Reforms unconstitutional because they provided excessive government control of industry

C. Open Market Committee was formed as a private board to make monetary policy

Questions

1. What are pieces of eight?

2. What is a Bill of Credit?

3. What was the difference between the Gold Eagle and the Silver Dollar?

4. Why did Article 1 section 8 of the United States Constitution provide an economic advantage for the United States?

5. What was the effect of the Legal Tender Act of 1862?

_____

_____

_____

6. What was the significance of the Supreme Court decision in *Knox v. Lee*, (1871) and *Julliard v. Greenman* (1884)?

_____

_____

_____

7. What is the danger of a fractional reserve system of banking?

_____

_____

_____

8. Why did the Government seize gold from the American public under Franklin D. Roosevelt?

_____

_____

_____

9. Why is the Judicial System and Congress a poor means of attempting to reform the national monetary system?

_____

_____

_____

10. Why is it important for the Christian statesman to study economics, especially as it relates to the monetary system?

_____

_____

_____

Further Reading

In 1832, Andrew Jackson vetoed a bill, putting an end to the Second National Bank. Jackson saw the Bank as an unconstitutional monopoly in which the special interests of the rich were accommodated by acts of Congress to exploit the poor. Upon issuing the veto of the bill Andrew Jackson made the following comments:

> *"I sincerely regret that in the act before me [to renew the Bank of the United States] I can perceive none of those modifications of the bank charter which are necessary, in my opinion, to make it compatible with justice, with sound policy, or with the Constitution of our country.*
>
> *The Bank of the United States enjoys an exclusive privilege of banking under the authority of the General Government . . . . The powers, privileges, and favors bestowed upon it in the original charter, by increasing the value of the stock far above its par value, operated as a gratuity of many millions to the stock-holders. . . .*
>
> *Every monopoly and all exclusive privileges are granted at the expense of the public, which ought to receive a fair equivalent. The many millions which this act proposes to bestow on the stockholders of the existing bank must come directly or indirectly out of the earnings of the American people. It is due to them, therefore, if their Government sell monopolies and exclusive privileges, that they should at least exact for them as much as they are worth in open market. . . .But this act does not permit competition in the purchase of this monopoly. It seems to be predicated on the erroneous idea that the present stockholders have a prescriptive right not only to the favor but to the bounty of Government.*
>
> *It is to be regretted that the rich and powerful too often bend the acts of government to their selfish purposes. Distinctions in society will always exist under every just government. Equality of talents, of education, or of wealth can not be produced by human institutions.*

In the full enjoyment of the gifts of Heaven and the fruits of superior industry, economy, and virtue, every man is equally entitled to protection by law; but when the laws undertake to add to these natural and just advantages artificial distinctions, to grant titles, gratuities, and exclusive privileges, to make the rich richer and the potent more powerful, the humble members of society the farmers, mechanics, and laborers who have neither the time nor the means of securing like favors to themselves, have a right to complain of the injustice of their Government. . . .

Most of the difficulties our Government now encounters and most of the dangers which impend over our Union have sprung from an abandonment of the legitimate objects of Government by our national legislation, and the adoption of such principles as are embodied in this act. Many of our rich men have not been content with equal protection and equal benefits, but have besought us to make them richer by act of Congress. By attempting to gratify their desires we have in the results of our legislation arrayed section against section, interest against interest, and man against man, in a fearful commotion which threatens to shake the foundations of our Union."

Definitions

Fiat Money: Currency offered as legal tender yet has no true value.

Legal Tender: Coins or bank notes that must be accepted if offered in the payment of debts.

Bill of Credit: A written instrument requiring the issuer to exchange the written instrument for value at a specified time.

Writing Assignment

There is much debate about the excessive spending by the Federal Government on special interests that do not tend to benefit private citizens. Read the address given by Andrew Jackson in 1832, as he brought down the Second Bank of the United States. Write at least 500 words about his attitude toward the poor, the Constitution, monopolies, and use of tax dollars to fund special interests. Include in your discussion his attitude toward equality and social welfare. How do you think he would react to our Government enterprises today?

Recommendations for Further Study

Pieces of Eight, by Edwin Vieira

The Constitutional of the United States with Index, by U.S. Government

The Mystery of Banking, by Murray Rothbard

Larceny in the Heart, by R.J. Rushdoony

Introduction to Christian Economics, by Gary North

Unit Four

Unit Four–Lesson 1
Federalism and Safeguards Against Democracy

Introduction

During the summer of 1788, the State of Virginia was debating the ratification of the new Federal Constitution. Patrick Henry expressed his grave concerns that a federal government may over time war against the sovereign authority of the states. He predicted that eventually the Federal Government would exceed its constitutional authority and asserts a general power over the free and independent states absorbing all state power under the arm of a central federal government. This usurpation of state authority was doomed to lead to either a break-up of the federal union between the states or would lead to a loss of state independence and with it the rights of the people to govern themselves according to the demands of their conscience and local jurisdictions.

In an effort to alleviate Henry's concern and those of the assembly, Edmund Pendleton, a member of the Virginia Convention, assured the assembly:

> *"I believe I am still correct, and insist that, if each power is confined within its proper bounds, and to its proper objects, an interference*

can never happen. Being for two different purposes, as long as they
are limited to the different objects, they can no more clash than two
parallel lines can meet. . . ."[32]

Of course Mr. Pendleton was right; if each power was restricted to the proper bounds of its constituted authority there would be no conflict between federal and state power. However, Patrick Henry's fears have been realized as the right to local self-government among the states is being aggressively subverted. In fact, these attacks have sought to destroy the republican form of government, which is guaranteed by the Constitution of the United States, and to replace it with democracy.

It has become increasingly popular to refer to the United States' as being a Democracy. However, the United States are not a Democracy. In fact, the founding fathers were critical of examples of Grecian democracy. James Monroe found the constitutions of ancient Greece to be seriously flawed and not to be trusted by Americans. Alexander Hamilton, John Jay, and James Madison each agreed that the ancient democracies of Greece were turbulent and were, unfit for the imitation, as they are repugnant to the genius of America. John Adams while critically examining twelve ancient democratic republics and found them "all inferior to the political system of the new American republics in the several states. . . ."[33]

America is a Constitutionally Federated Republic. Each state retains its own sovereignty, but is federated with others states under the United States constitution, which in turn guarantees a republic form of government in each state. The nature of federalism and republicanism are not complementary since they prevent one majoritarian group of people or states to exercise authority over a minority group of people or states. Moreover, civil magistrates are elected from among the people, not as representatives of the people, but as representatives of the constitution and the laws of the land. The Electoral College was established as an asset to maintain the strict lines of federalism between the Federal Government and the States. This allows for less populated states the full representative power of more populated state, allowing for each state to play an equal role in the federal union of states.

There have been efforts from the time of America's founding to brake down these lines of federalism. One example was the ratification of the seventeenth amendment, which removed the authority of the state governments to be represented in the federal senate, the House of Representatives being the people's house. Prior to the ratification of the seventeenth amendment the senate was composed of member elected among the state legislators. The seventeenth amendment removed the ability of State Legislators to elect senators to congress, and in its place established a popular election from among the people. The seventeenth amendment was a subversion of republicanism and a move toward pure democracy.

In addition, there has been no small amount of criticism of the Electoral College. Some have suggested that the Electoral College should be dispensed of, and that presidential elections should be purely democratic. This of course would cause an unbalanced in the representation among lesser populated states and minority populations. In addition, it would further break down the wall of divided sovereignty between the federal government and the states.

In this lecture, Howard Phillips will walk you through the history of the Electoral College and will explain the essential nature of the Electoral College in maintaining federalism, republicanism, and our right to local self-government.

Lecture Outline

1. The Qualifications to Be President of the United States

A. Must be born a natural born in the United States

B. Must be 35 years of age or older

2. The Electoral College

A. There are 538 electors in the electoral college

B. The State Legislatures decide the manner in which electors are appointed in their states

3. Federalism

A. Federalism was built into the electoral process by America's Founders

B. Federalism was substantially undermined by the 17th amendment

4. The Nature Electoral College at Work

A. The electors may vote for anyone they choose

B. If a candidate dies after the popular elections, but prior to the beginning of the term the electors may elect the next president of the United States

5. The Election of 1800

A. The vote in the Electoral College was tied

B. The vote then went to Congress and each state had one vote. A majority of the states (at that time 16) were needed for victory

C. 35 ballots were cast in the house without an outcome to the election

D. As a result of the tie Congress passed the twelfth amendment

6. The Election of 1824

A. In 1824 Andrew Jackson had a larger number of popular votes than John Quincy Adams, but did not have a majority of the electors

B. The election went to the House of Representatives

C. Henry Clay threw his votes in the House of Representatives to John Quincy Adams and the election was stolen from Jackson

7. The Election of 1876

A. Samuel B. Tildon was elected president, but it was stolen from him when the electorates in the south voted for Rutherford B. Hays

8. How to Win an Election with Only One Electoral Vote

A. A majority in the electoral college is 270 votes

B. If one candidate received 269 and another candidate received 268, but the remaining vote went to a third party, it would go to the House of Representatives, and the third party could win

9. How the Speaker of the House is Acting President

A. If the houses of Congress failed to gather the necessary two-thirds majority needed to vote, there would be no president or vice president elect.

B. In that case the Speaker of the House would become acting president until the presidency was determined

Questions

1. When is the President Elected by the Electors?

_____

_____

_____

2. How many presidential elections are there every four years?

    _____

    _____

    _____

3. How does the Electoral College guard against fraud in an election?

    _____

    _____

    _____

4. How did the 17th Amendment to the United States Constitution diminish federalism in the electoral process?

    _____

    _____

    _____

5. How did the Election of 1800 change how elections were decided?

    _____

    _____

    _____

6. Why did Henry Clay give his votes to John Quincy Adams in the House of Representatives in the Election of 1824?

    _____

    _____

    _____

7. Why did the electorates in the South vote for Rutherford B. Hays, even though Samuel Tildon had won the election of 1876?

_____

_____

_____

8. How could a president be elected by just one electoral vote?

_____

_____

_____

9. How could the speaker of the house become acting president in an election without entering the election as a candidate?

_____

_____

_____

10. What would be the consequence if the Electoral College were abolished?

_____

_____

_____

Selected Reading

Early English kings took an oath of office which was representative of their faith in Christ and their duty to the subjects in their realm. The Coronation oath of Edgar in 946 is recorded as follows:

> *"In the name of the Holy Trinity I promise three things to the Christian People my subjects: First, that God's church and all Christian people in my realm shall enjoy true peace; Second, that I*

forbid all ranks of men robbery and all wrongful deeds; Third, that I urge and command justice and mercy in all judgment, so that the gracious ad compassionate God who lives and reigns may grant us all His everlasting Mercy."

Definitions

Democracy: A system of popular sovereignty in government by the whole population or all the eligible members of the state.

Republic: A system of government in which a representative is elected to represent fixed constitutional principles.

Federalism: A system in which many states unite for a limited common purpose, but maintain their own internal sovereignty.

Electoral College: A body of electors chosen by the states to represent the various states in the national election of a President and Vice President.

Writing Assignment

The importance of the Federalism might be illustrated by the Public Transportation system in California. The legislature unilaterally passed legislation requiring every county to establish and maintain a public transportation system. Most well populated metropolitan areas already had a public transportation system, yet smaller less populated counties were forced to allocate scarce funds to maintain a public transportation system that is never used. The Federalism offered a wall of protections from the same imprudent measures from being imposed by the Federal Government. In at least 500 words, write an essay contrasting the needs in rural areas to those in urban areas. Include a discussion of the importance of the founders emphasis on local self-government.

Recommendations for Further Study

The Importance of the Electoral College, by George Grant

The Establishment and Limits of Civil Government, by James Wilson

Lives of the Presidents of the United States, by John Abbot

The Roots of the American Republic, by E.C. Wines

Unit Four–Lesson 2
Women's Roles in Politics

Introduction

During the past century the role of women in the political process has been an issue of great debate. The rise of feminism, the break down of the family, and the abdication of men from roles of leadership have all contributed to an increasing number of women who desire to serve in the role of civil magistrate. Unfortunately, most Christians have been guided by cultural norms and have not sought to be instructed by Scripture as to what the proper role of women is in the political process.

Without a doubt women are citizens of the state and are vested with all of the rights, liberties, and protections that are afforded to men. Moreover, in the debate of political jurisdiction, there should not be any general question of the practical ability of women in carrying out such a role. Rather the consideration should be what Bible say about the role of women in matters of civil government. In the thirty-first chapters of Proverbs, we are provided with the biblical ideal for a woman. We find that she is married, has children, and is a keeper at home. She is intelligent, highly skilled, industrious, prudent, and active in her community. However, with regard to the civil rule we read in verse twenty-three, "Her husband is known in the gates, when he sitteth among the elders of the land." As a helper to her husband, she is praised in this passage for her husband's role as a civil ruler in the land. In terms of the role of women in the civil realm she is not to seek civil office, but rather carry out her role in her home and in her community as a help suitable to her husband. Elsewhere, in Titus 2:4-5 we are taught that older women should, "teach the young women to be sober, to love their husbands, to love their children, to be discreet, chaste, keepers at home, good, obedient to their own husbands, that the word of God be not blasphemed." In other words, the Scripture plainly bears out that a social norm in which women are not keepers at home and rule over their husbands is an affront to the commandments of God.

This blasphemy of the Word of God might be illustrated by considering commandments such as that found in Ephesians 5: 22 -24:

> *"Wives, submit yourselves unto your own husbands, as unto the Lord. For the husband is the head of the wife, even as Christ is the head of the church: and he is the savior of the body. Therefore as the church is subject unto Christ, so let the wives be to their own husbands in every thing."*

If a wife is to be subject to her husband in every thing as the Scripture requires, it would be impossible for a women to demand civil obedience from her husband and at the same time obey her husband in everything. The very exercise of her civil prerogative against her husband would be a violation of this precept.

Yet, many Christians have made vigorous efforts to justify the role of women as civil magistrates in spite of the clear teaching of Scripture. Instead, many will point to women such as Lydia in Acts chapter sixteen or Dorcas in Acts chapter nine as examples of women who held positions of authority outside of the home. However, a careful examination of these passages will prove that the claims misrepresent these women and the Scripture.

In Acts 16:14-15, we find:

> *"A certain woman named Lydia, a seller of purple, of the city of Thyatira, which worshipped God, heard us: whose heart the Lord opened, that she attended unto the things which were spoken of Paul. And when she was baptized, and her household, she besought us, saying, if ye have judged me to be faithful to the Lord, come into my house, and abide there. And she constrained us."*

From the outset, it is clear that Lydia is a seller of purple, not a "civil magistrate." She was obviously not married, and was not a Christian at the time she is introduced. Her profession is not political in nature but domestic. In Acts 9:36, we find "a certain disciple named Tabitha, which by interpretation is called Dorcas: this woman was full of good works and alms deeds which she did." Tabitha was a disciple (a title assumed by all Christians during that time). She was full of good works and alms deeds. Again, there is no evidence that she was a civil leader or had a profession outside of the home.

Finally, there are many who point to the example of Deborah in the book of Judges. However, there are several reasons why Deborah fails to establish a normative example for women who serve as civil magistrates. First, she was a prophetess who gave counsel under a tree and not in a traditional seat of authority. Second, we find Deborah was not called to deliver Israel, but rather God told Deborah to call Barak. Third, we find in Judges 5:12, that there were others at the time who carried out the duties of civil governors over Israel during the time of Deborah. Finally, even if Deborah can be properly considered a civil magistrate, it must be considered as an example of God's judgment on Israel.[34]

In this lecture, William Einwechter will confront this very timely issue. He will explain that from creation God has established a system of order and authority which man cannot change. Moreover, he will explain that while they are not permitted to assume positions of leadership, women play a vital role in the functioning of the church, family, and civil government. Finally, Mr. Einwechter will expound on the importance for the Christian statesman to understand the biblical standards for selecting a civil magistrate prior to casting his vote.

Lecture Outline

1. The Bible Speaks of Three Things That Indicate a Judgment on the Land

    A. The death of the innocent

    B. Moral perversion

    C. Women ruling over men

2. Why Cover This Subject

    A. Because it is closely related to the heresy of feminism

    B. Because the Bible speaks directly to this issue

    C. The current circumstance in which more women are going into politics

3. It is not Biblically Permissible for Women to Serve as Civil Magistrates

    A. The Doctrine of male headship applies to each government institution

   B.   The biblical qualifications for civil rulers forbid female magistrates

   C.   The biblical role of women is against the practice of female magistrates

   D.   The biblical lament of women ruling over men is also against female magistrates

   E.   The biblical example of Deborah is not an endorsement of female magistrates

4. The Bible is the Authoritative Standard of all Faith and Practice

5. The Blast of the Trumpet Against the Monstrous Regiment of Women

   A.   At the time this tract was written four civil ruling women opposed the Reformation: Catherine de Medici of France, Mary Tutor, Marie Deloraine, Mary Queen of Scots, Mary Tudor.

   B.   The Christian opposition is not based on the supposed weakness of women but what the Bible has to say

6. The Biblical Doctrine of Headship

   A.   God is a God of order

   B.   Men are going to share in God's government by ruling under His authority

      i.   Family: the husband has authority over his family

      ii.   Church: elders have authority in the local church

      iii.   State: the civil government has authority over those within a civil jurisdiction

7. I Corinthians 11:3

   A.   Christ is the supreme authority

   B.   The head of man is Christ

   C.   The head of woman is the man

   D.   This is an universal order established at Creation

8. The Qualifications of a Civil Magistrate

   A.   All magistrates are God's servants

   B.   The Scripture commands us to place men over us

   C.   We must elect wise men of understanding

D. Proven character

E. Must fear God

9. The Biblical Role of the Woman is Opposed to the Idea of Female Magistrates

A. The woman was created to be a helper suited for man

B. She is called to fulfill the roles that God has determined for her

C. She is to be a keeper at home

D. She is to be the mother of children

10. The Lament of Scripture Concerning Female Magistrates

A. Isaiah 3:12: It is a sign of judgment when women become Civil Magistrates

B. The men of Judah were weak and incompetent, not fearing God

11. Deborah is Not a Biblical Justification for Female Civil Magistrates

A. We are never to allow our culture to interpret the Scripture

B. God did not call Deborah, but instead told Deborah to call Barack

C. Deborah recognized that she was a mere advisor to the Civil Magistrates in Israel

12. The Importance of a Biblical Standard for Voting

A. It is important in the battle against feminism and egalitarianism

B. If we are not consistent on this issue, we lose the ability to make the same application in the church and the family.

C. We must avoid the sin of disobeying the Word of God

Questions

1. What are the three God ordained institutions?

_____

_____

_____

2. Who wrote *The First Blast of the Trumpet Against the Monstrous Regiment of Women*?

_____

_____

_____

3. What is the doctrine of headship?

_____

_____

_____

4. What is the significance of 1 Corinthians 11:3?

_____

_____

_____

5. What are the qualifications of civil magistrates?

_____

_____

_____

6. Why is the Creation important to the issue of women serving as female magistrates?

_____

_____

_____

7. How does the role of women, as defined by Scripture, preclude a woman from serving as a civil magistrate?

_____

_____

_____

8. What is the attitude in Scripture toward seasons when women served as civil magistrates?

_____

_____

_____

9. Why is Deborah a poor example for justifying women serving as female magistrates?

_____

_____

_____

10. Why is this battle for the biblical role of women in the civil sphere important to our modern culture?

_____

_____

_____

Further Reading

In his *First Blast of the Trumpet Against the Monstrous Regiment of Women*, John Knox explains that the rule of women over the civil realm is contrary to the design set forth in Scripture:

> *"I say, that woman in her greatest perfection was made to serve and*

obey man, not to rule and command him. As St. Paul does reason in these words: Man is not of the woman, but the woman of the man. And man was not created for the cause of the woman, but the woman for the cause of man; and therefore ought the woman to have a power upon her head (that is, a cover in sign of subjection). Of which words it is plain that the apostle means, that woman in her greatest perfection should have known that man was lord above her; and therefore that she should never have pretended any kind of superiority above him, no more than do the angels above God the Creator, or above Christ their head. So I say, that in her greatest perfection, woman was created to be subject to man.

But after her fall and rebellion committed against God, there was put upon her a new necessity, and she was made subject to man by the irrevocable sentence of God, pronounced in these words: I will greatly multiply thy sorrow and thy conception. With sorrow shalt thou bear thy children, and thy will shall be subject to thy man; and he shall bear dominion over thee (Gen. 3:16). Hereby may such as altogether be not blinded plainly see, that God by his sentence has dejected all women from empire and dominion above man. For two punishments are laid upon her: to wit, a dolour, anguish, and pain, as oft as ever she shall be mother; and a subjection of her self, her appetites, and will, to her husband, and to his will. From the former part of this malediction can neither art, nobility, policy, nor law made by man deliver womankind; but whosoever attains to that honour to be mother, proves in experience the effect and strength of God's word. But (alas!) ignorance of God, ambition, and tyranny have studied to abolish and destroy the second part of God's punishment. For women are lifted up to be heads over realms, and to rule above men at their pleasure and appetites. But horrible is the vengeance which is prepared for the one and for the other, for the promoters and for the persons promoted, except they speedily repent. For they shall be dejected from the glory of the sons of God to the slavery of the devil, and to the torment that is prepared for all such as do exalt themselves against God."

Definitions

Regiment: The term regiment used by Knox means civil rule.

Feminism: A movement against the traditional family and the biblical role of women in which groups of women sought to deny the biblical doctrine of headship and remove it from every aspect of society.

Hierarchy: A concept concerning who God has delegated authority to in a particular sphere of human government.

Headship: Headship involves the order God has established in every sphere of government in which the head is the covenant representative of those over whom he has authority.

Writing Assignment

In the United States Supreme Court Decision, *Bradwell v. Illinois* the court held that the constitution of the family organization is founded in the divine ordinance. The paramount mission and destiny of women is to fulfill the noble offices of wife and mother. This is the Law of the Creator, and the rules of civil society must be adapted to the general constitution of things. Since that time, the feminist movement has aggressively sought to eradicate every vestige of this divine ordinance on society. The feminist movement has led to abortions on demand, no fault divorce, symbolic speech, and the general breakdown of the family. In at least 500 words, write an essay describing the importance of maintaining biblical gender roles in society. Include in your discussion some of the modern-day consequences for having abandoned God's establishment of order in this area.

Recommendations for Further Study

The First Blast of the Trumpet Against the Monstrous Regiment of Women, by John Knox

Killer Angel, by George Grant

Passionate Housewives, Desperate for God, by Jennie Chancey and Stacy McDonald

Unit Five

Unit 5–Lesson 1
The Executive Branch

Introduction

The Executive branch of the Federal Government has far reaching authority, which is "vested in a President of the United States of America."[35] During the ratification of the Federal Constitution some argued that too much power had been given to the President of the United States, and that the Federal Constitution would create the office of a sort of king. In response to this argument, Alexander Hamilton wrote Federalist Paper 69, which distinguished the presidency from a monarchy.

Hamilton pointed out that, unlike a monarchy, the President was to serve for a limited term and could be impeached and removed from office. The President's veto may be overridden by the two/thirds vote in Congress and has not authority to declare war, tax the people, or make new laws. The president is a public servant who's authority and office is limited to enforcing the laws passed by Congress, defending the Constitution, and protecting the nation from enemies foreign and domestic. The end result, argued Hamilton, was that the President of the United States did not have any more authority than that afforded to the power vested in the state governors under the various states' constitutions; and, in some cases the state governors were said to have more authority.

Yet, the power of the Executive has been expanded to areas not granted in the Constitution, in ways that make the President much more like a monarch that an executive. Furthermore, this extreme subversion of the constitutional limitations placed on the Executive office have been ignored and even defended by the United States Congress, the Supreme Court, and the States. The constitutional authority of the Executive Branch, although great, is restricted to a number of delineable areas of executive power:

(1) The President of the United States serves as Commander and Chief of the armed forces and the militias of the several states when called into service. However, the President has no constitutional authority to declare or engage in foreign or domestic wars. The war power is reserved exclusively to Congress.

(2) In addition, as protector of the United States Constitution, the President has the authority to grant reprieves and pardon for offenses against the United States. However, the pardon power, under the Constitution, only extends to federal crimes, and not to state crimes. Neither may the President offer a reprieve or pardon in matters of impeachment.

(3) The President of the United States has the authority to engage in matters of foreign policy, receive foreign officers and ambassadors, and may sign treaties with foreign nations. Yet, this power is shared with the United States Congress and treaties must be ratified by two-thirds of the Senate before a treaty is binding or enforceable.

(4) The President of the United States has the authority to appoint ambassadors, public ministers, federal judges, consuls, and other officers of the United States. However, these appointments must be made with the advice of, and confirmed with a majority vote of, the United States Senate. Congress may also vest the appointment of inferior officers in any official branch or office of government, as they deem appropriate.

(5) The President has the power to commission officers to fill vacancies that occur during the recess of the Senate. The commissions expire at the end of the following congressional session.

(6) The President also has what is sometimes referred to as the power of persuasion. He must present himself before Congress and give account for the state of the Union. During this time he may recommend that the Congress consider measures that he judges to be necessary and expedient. In addition, in extraordinary circumstances he may convene the houses of Congress for a special session. However, the President has no legislative authority and may only seek to persuade Congress to pass legislation that is necessary and expedient.

(7) The President has a power of veto any legislation that poses a threat to the state of the Union or which is deemed unconstitutional. However, the veto effectively returns the legislation to Congress for further consideration. The President's veto may be overruled by a two-thirds vote in Congress.

(8) Finally, the President is obligated to see that the laws passed by Congress are faithfully executed. However, this authority is limited to executing the laws which have already been passed by Congress and signed into law by the President. An Executive Order has no legislative authority.

In this lecture, former presidential candidate, Howard Phillips, will discuss the framework of a constitutional presidency. He will explain how the constitutional limitations on the President's authority have been diluted and in many cases have been abandoned. Finally, Mr. Phillips will explain why it is important that the Christian statesman understand the constitutional nature of the Executive Office.

Lecture Outline

1. Disregard of the Constitutional Provisions for the Executive Branch

    A. There is no unlimited grant of authority given to the President of the United States

2. Right Under the Declaration of Independence

    A. God is sovereign and law is the will of the sovereign

    B. Man is accountable to God being His creation

    C. God gave us certain unalienable rights

3. The Constitution of the United States Article One Section One

    A. Congress is the only branch of government that has the authority of legislation

4. Executive Orders

    A. A president may issue an executive order that seeks to implement policy enacted by Congress.

    B. An executive order may not be used constitutionally as a means of passing legislation

5. Regulatory Agencies

A. Regulatory agencies often impose policies that go beyond what Congress has legislated

6. Civil Service Personnel

A. Civil service personnel have a tenured position and set policies that go beyond what Congress has permitted through legislation

7. Government Programs

A. Government programs are allowed to exist and operate unconstitutionally and implement benefits and detriments to the public without an act of Congress

8. International Bureaucracies

A. The United Nations, the International Monetary Fund, and the World Bank are all international bureaucracies that have been allowed to implement policies in the United States without an act of Congress.

B. Only Congress may constitutionally regulate commerce with foreign nations

9. The Federal Reserve Bank

A. The Federal Reserve Bank, a private banking group, has been able to set monetary policy and print currency in the United States.

B. Andrew Jackson, a heroic president

C. By devaluing savings and earnings the Federal Reserve acts as a taxing instrument

10. The Supreme Court in *Roe v. Wade*

A. 5 of 7 members of the court were Republicans

B. A president would have the authority to end abortion

11. Impoundment

A. A president has the power to impound money if he believes the money is being spent for an unconstitutional purpose

B. The President can also withhold funding for a court that rules unconstitutionally

12. The Problem of Incrementalism

A. Incrementalism is a denial of swift justice and allows evil to spread

Questions

1. What are the two principles on which our nation is founded?

    _____

    _____

    _____

2. What rights does the Declaration of Independence enumerate as unalienable?

    _____

    _____

    _____

3. How are executive orders limited?

    _____

    _____

    _____

4. How are Civil Service Personnel permitted to obstruct the constitutional political process?

    _____

    _____

    _____

5. How is the North American Free Trade Agreement an abdication of congressional authority?

_____

_____

_____

6. How could the President end the practice of abortion in the United States?

_____

_____

_____

7. Why should Christians be wary of aligning with a certain political party?

_____

_____

_____

8. Why is the Federal Reserve unconstitutional?

_____

_____

_____

9. Why is it so difficult for a third party to successfully run for the presidency?

_____

_____

_____

10. What is the problem with Incrementalism?

_____

_____

_____

Selected Reading

Alexander Hamilton defends the office of the Constitutional Executive in Federalist number sixty-nine:

> "The first thing which strikes our attention is, that the executive authority, with few exceptions, is to be vested in a single magistrate. This will scarcely, however, be considered as a point upon which any comparison can be grounded; for if, in this particular, there be a resemblance to the king of Great Britain, there is not less a resemblance to the Grand Seignior, to the khan of Tartary, to the Man of the Seven Mountains, or to the governor of New York.
>
> That magistrate is to be elected for four years; and is to be re-eligible as often as the people of the United States shall think him worthy of their confidence.... If we consider how much less time would be requisite for establishing a dangerous influence in a single State, than for establishing a like influence throughout the United States, we must conclude that a duration of four years for the Chief Magistrate of the Union is a degree of permanency far less to be dreaded in that office, than a duration of three years for a corresponding office in a single State.
>
> Hence it appears that, except as to the concurrent authority of the President in the article of treaties, it would be difficult to determine whether that magistrate would, in the aggregate, possess more or less power than the Governor of New York. And it appears yet more unequivocally, that there is no pretense for the parallel which has been attempted between him and the king of Great Britain."

Definitions

Incrementalism: A system in which an individual attempts to make changes by degrees.

Impoundment: A political doctrine in which a president may seize items that are allocated for an unconstitutional purpose.

Writing Assignment

There are many who argue that an executive must not force his religion on the society. Yet, the office of the executive is established to enforce the moral prerogatives passed by Congress on the same individuals who reject such morality. Consider how the Department of Housing and Human Services imposes a religious ethic by forcing a commercial property owner to rent space to an abortion clinic, or force a Christian couple to rent their second home to homosexuals. Consider the Department of Labor who forces Christians to hire women against their conscience. Such laws are based on a religious system of ethics and are enforced whether or not you profess faith in that ethical system or not. In at least 500 words, write an essay discussing at least one area in which laws are enforced on the basis of a religious social norm. In your answer discuss how you think current political leaders might justify this hypocrisy. Finally, what is the Executive's moral obligation to the Word of God? Does this obligation transcend the duties of his office?

Recommendations for Further Study

Lives of the Presidents of the United States, by John Abbot

George Washington's Sacred Fire, by Peter A. Lillback

Life of Andrew Jackson, by John Jenkins

The Founder Constitution, Editor, Philip B. Kurland and Ralph Lerner

Unit Six

Unit Six–Lesson 1
The Judicial Branch

Introduction

The Supreme Court has become one of the most powerful and certainly the most instrumental in subverting the Constitution along with the rights and liberties of the entire nation. The Judicial Branch of the United States today is clearly not the Judicial Branch that the framers of the United Sates had envisioned. This might be illustrated by looking at what the founding fathers had envisioned.

> *"Whoever attentively considers the different departments of power must perceive, that, in a government in which they are separated from each other, the judiciary, from the nature of its functions, will always be the least dangerous to the political rights of the Constitution; because it will be least in a capacity to annoy or injure them. The Executive not only dispenses the honors, but holds the sword of the community. The legislature not only commands the purse, but prescribes the rules by which the duties and rights of every citizen are to be regulated. The judiciary, on the contrary, has no influence over either the sword or the purse; no direction either of the strength or of the wealth of the society; and can take no active resolution whatever. It may truly be*

said to have neither FORCE nor WILL, but merely judgment; and
must ultimately depend upon the aid of the executive arm even for the
efficacy of its judgments." [36]

First of all, there is only one court established under the Constitution, and that is the Supreme Court. All inferior federal courts have been created under the powers of Congress under Article 3 Section 1 and Article 1 Section 8 of the United States Constitution. These inferior courts may be removed or restructured by acts of Congress.

The Supreme Court doesn't have power to pass legislation or even to enforce its own judgments. The court must rely on Congress to legislate and on the Executive to enforce its judgments. The Supreme Court only has a limited jurisdiction to issue a judgment in a limited number of areas. These areas within the court's limited jurisdiction are:

(1) Cases arising under the Constitution, federal laws, and treaties;

(2) Cases involving diplomats such as ambassadors and other public ministers;

(3) Cases in which the United States is suing or being sued;

(4) Cases involving admiralty and maritime disputes;

(5) Conflicts between two or more states, or citizens from different states;

(6) Conflicts arising under certain land grants between states and citizens of foreign jurisdictions;

(7) The court has appellate jurisdiction over issues of law and fact, but is limited in this jurisdiction by laws that Congress shall pass.

Moreover, the manner in which the court arrives at a judgment is limited to considerations of the Constitution of the United States, the laws of Congress, and treaties ratified by Congress. Their consideration may not constitutionally extend to considerations of foreign law or changing social norms, as has been the practice among modern courts. The Constitution offers safeguards to prevent the judiciary from exceeding its lawful authority. As Hamilton pointed out:

"According to the plan of the convention, all judges who may be appointed
by the United States are to hold their offices during good behavior…
. The standard of good behavior for the continuance in office of the
judicial magistracy, is certainly one of the most valuable of the modern
improvements in the practice of government. In a monarchy it is an
excellent barrier to the despotism of the prince; in a republic it is a no less
excellent barrier to the encroachments and oppressions of the representative
body. And it is the best expedient which can be devised in any government,
to secure a steady, upright, and impartial administration of the laws." [37]

In other words, a Supreme Court justice who attempts to legislate or enforce his judgments, appeals to foreign law, or changing social norms, who is partial and oppressive, or who undermines the United States Constitution has violated his office and should be removed to maintain the integrity of the judiciary and the legal profession.

In this lecture, William Einwechter will explain why it is important for judges to have a biblical framework of law. He will explain the differences between various views of law and jurisprudence and will explain why only nations which observe a biblical framework for law and jurisprudence can have any hope for order, justice, and integrity among the judiciary.

Lecture Outline

1. Doug Phillips Introduction

2. The Importance of Having a Biblical View of Law and Politics

3. The Rejection of the Old Testament Law

4. Jurisprudence (What is Law?)

A. Latin words: *juris*=of law; *prudence*=knowledge, skill

B. The study of the nature, content, and purpose of law

5. Christian Jurisprudence

A. Seeks to answer the same questions from a Christian perspective

B. Based on the revelation of Jesus Christ

C. Based on the presupposition that:

   i. The Word of God is the only infallible source of truth

   ii. The Triune God is the Creator of all things and Sovereign Lord of all things

6. Defining Positive Law

A. Refers to law that is actually and specifically enacted by proper authority for the government of society; the law of the State

B. Descriptive rather then prescriptive

C. Separation between law and morals

      i.   Law is social and objective while morals are individual and subjective

      ii. Law is coercive while morals are voluntary

      iii. Law is external command while morals induce internal motivation.

D. Two theories of law:

      i.   The historical school of law: law is exclusively the product of public consciousness and evolution

      ii. The school of legal positivism: the only law valid is the one that can be empirically verified

E. Reasons why legal positivism loses ground

F. Positive law is diametrically opposed to Christian Jurisprudence

G. Legal insights of Positive Law of assistance to Christian Jurisprudence

      i.   Law is the will of a sovereign power

      ii. Law can be verified in an objective way

7. Natural Law

A. Definition: Blackstone Commentaries

B. Principle of natural law:

      i.   "Unchanging principles of law that exist in nature"

      ii. Accessible to all men and discovered by right use of reason

      iii. Applies to all men at all times and in all circumstances

      iv. Eminent in human nature

      v. Man-made laws are just and authoritative if derivable from the principles in nature

C. History of natural law

      i.   Classical era: based on Greeks and Romans; paganism

      ii. Medieval era: Roman Catholic Church; scholastic, syncretism

      iii. Modern era: naturalistic, individualistic, radical; French revolution; deism

D. The three schools of natural law

      i.   Classical: Greek idealism and stoicism

      ii. Medieval: scholasticism

      iii. Modern: humanism and naturalism

8. **General Revelation: God's Revelation through the Natural World he Created**

9. **Special Revelation: God's Revelation through His Word**

10. **God Made Man With the Capacity for Moral Judgment and a Knowledge of Him and His Moral Law**

11. **Effects of Sin**

   A. Epistemological effect: the prideful assumption that man can know good and evil apart from God's word

   B. Moral effect: suppressing the truth (Romans 1)

12. **The Essence of Greek Natural Law Theory: To Be Like God**

13. **Romans 2:13,14**

14. **A Critique of Natural Law Theory**

   A. Born in the womb of human rebellion

   B. Denied man's need for God's special revelation

   C. Minimizes the effect of the fall

   D. It is not in the Scriptures

   E. Contrary to the biblical concept of Torah

   F. Denies the full sufficiency and authority of Scripture

   G. No defined content

   H. Not a part of the Church's commission to disciple the nations

   I. Aspect of the vain philosophies Christian should cast down: 2 Corinthians 10:3-5; Colossians 2:8

15. **Reasons Given by Christians Embracing Natural Law**

   A. Provides a point of contact with unbelievers

   B. Provides a higher law to judge the law of State

16. **The Law of God, the Only Foundation for Christian Jurisprudence**

17. Four Points on the Authority of Biblical Law

A. Sovereignty of Scriptures; Daniel 4, Psalm 2

B. The sufficiency of Scriptures; Psalm 19:7-10; 2 Timothy 3:15-17

C. Judgment is God's; Deuteronomy 1:16-17

D. All Old Testament is good; 1 Timothy 1:8-11

18. Conclusion: What is Law?

Questions

1. What is Jurisprudence?

_____

_____

_____

2. What presupposition is a Christian view of jurisprudence based on?

_____

_____

_____

3. What is positive Law?

_____

_____

_____

4. What is law according to the modern school of legal theory?

    _____

    _____

    _____

5. What is legal positivism?

    _____

    _____

    _____

6. Can there be any ethical neutrality to law?

    _____

    _____

    _____

7. What distinguishes Christian Jurisprudence from Positive Law?

    _____

    _____

    _____

8. What is Natural Law based on?

    _____

    _____

    _____

9. What are the three schools of Natural Law?

_____

_____

_____

10. What are special and general revelation?

_____

_____

_____

11. What is the epistemological effect of sin?

_____

_____

_____

12. Is Natural Law found in the Scriptures?

_____

_____

_____

Further Reading

Robert L. Dabney speaks about the Christian's duty toward God in the practice of the legal profession:

> *"The concern, which the country has in their professional integrity, and in their righteous and truthful exercise of these vast powers, is analogous to that which the church has in the orthodoxy of her ministers. Nor are these influences of the legal profession limited to things secular; for the domains of morals and religion so intermingle that the moral condition of a people, as to the duties of righteousness*

> *between, man and man, greatly influences their state towards God. It*
> *may well be doubted whether an acute and unprincipled bar does not*
> *do more to corrupt and ruin many communities than the pulpit does to*
> *sanctify and save them. These things at once justify the introduction of*
> *the topic into these discussions, and challenge the attention of Christian*
> *lawyers and readers to its great importance. . . ."*

Policy is not the test of right, on which side soever the advantage may lie; and we have too much faith in the immutable laws of rectitude, and in the providence of a holy God over human affairs, to believe that a true expediency is ever to be found in that which is immoral. In the final issue that which is right will always be found most expedient. . . .

And again, the State is as utterly devoid as the client of all right to misrepresent truth and right. God has given to the civil magistrate the right to slay murderers and invaders, but he has given to no person nor commonwealth under heaven the right to depart from the inexorable lines of truth and right. This great truth brings us back to the doctrine of each man's direct and unavoidable responsibility to God, for all his acts possessing moral character or moral consequences."[38]

Definitions

Positivism: an empirical theory of knowledge; natural science is the sum of human knowledge; rejects metaphysics

Metaphysics: the branch of philosophy that deals with the first principles of things, including abstract concepts such as being, knowing, cause, identity, time, and space

Syncretism: the mixture between paganism and Christian truths

Deism : the belief that God designed the world and left it to run by itself; no miracles or special revelation

Law : the will of the sovereign for his subjects

Writing Assignment

Clarence Darrow was an attorney early in the 20th century, renowned for his oratory skill to move judges and juries. Early in his career Darrow was a labor attorney, but after being charged with attempting to bribe juries he was forced to leave California, never to practice law there again. Later, Darrow took up criminal law and became known for defending some of the most immoral positions. In the

Scopes Trial, Darrow defended the theory of evolution in the public education. Moreover, he defended murderers Leopold and Loeb, on the basis that it was a case of survival of the fittest. Using what you have learned in this lesson, write a 500-word essay describing the influence that one person may have on the legal profession. Discuss how standing firm on an unpopular idea can ultimately lead to enormous results. Include in your discussion a contrast between wicked men like Darrow and the influence of godly men like John Witherspoon.

Recommendations for Further Study

The Institutes of Biblical Law, by R.J. Rushdoony

Law and Liberty, by R.J. Rushdoony

The Works of John Adams, by John Adams

Unit 6–Lesson 2
The Appointment of Godly Magistrates

Introduction

The Judicial Branch of the United States Government was thought by America's founders to be the most powerless branch of government. Yet, it was not thought to be the least important. The Supreme Court is a vital safeguard of liberty against the arbitrary powers of the legislature. A Supreme Court Justice is required to have mastery knowledge of a vast body of law and continue in constant study in order to carry out the functions of that office. Alexander Hamilton pointed out that there are only a few men in society, at any given time with the kind of mastery of the law requisite for a Supreme Court Justice. Even more, Hamilton pointed out, "Making the proper deductions for the ordinary depravity of human nature, the number must be still smaller of those who unite the requisite integrity with the requisite knowledge."[39]

Of course, Hamilton here summarizes the prerequisites for choosing civil magistrates in the Scripture. In the book of Exodus 18:21, God commands that judges be selected "from all the people able men, such as fear God, men of truth, hating covetousness;" and in Deuteronomy 1:13, "Take you wise men, and understanding, and known among your tribes, and I will make them rulers over you." Therefore, the biblical requirements confirm the criteria posited by Alexander Hamilton as to the type of men who are to be selected as judges. A judge must:

(1) Be a man;

(2) Must fear God;

(3) Be a man of truth;

(4) Hate covetousness;

(5) Have understanding;

(6) Must be known among his community.

These are the biblical requirements for the selection of any person desiring to hold civil office. Modernly, the president makes judicial appointments with the consent of Congress with little or no regard for any of these biblical criteria. Of course, this is to be expected, since a majority of Christians also ignore or outright reject this biblical criteria when casting their votes for the President and members of Congress. The consequences for not electing biblically qualified judges have been devastating.

One example of the devastating influences of unqualified judges who do not fear God nor regard the law can be illustrated by the Supreme Court's decision in *Griswold v. Connecticut* in 1965. In 1879, a law in Connecticut prohibited "any drug, medicinal article or instrument for the purpose of preventing conception." The law had been challenged several times, but was never successfully overturned until the late 20th century when the executive director of the Planned Parenthood League of Connecticut, Estelle Griswold was arrested for violating the statute. Griswold challenged the constitutionality of the statute in what became *Griswold v. Connecticut*. In 1965, Supreme Court Justice William O. Douglas found that a "right to privacy" which is not mentioned anywhere in the U.S. Constitution, was apparent in the "penumbras, formed by emanations" of the Constitution, and held that this smoke and mirrors approach was enough to rule the Connecticut statute unconstitutional.

The Supreme Courts ruling in Griswold opened the door to a plethora of pretended rights to engage in all sorts of immoral activity. Modern judges have used Griswold to find the right to practice sodomy in *Lawrence v. Texas*; and a mother's so-called right to murder her child, in *Roe v. Wade*. Modern courts have moved even further away from the Constitution by indiscriminately appealing to foreign law and changing social norms as grounds for finding new rights and discontinuing old ones. Simultaneously, courts have sought to remove every trace of Christianity from the public square and replace it with monuments to immorality. The Supreme Court in the United States has run out of control and the only remedy is to replace the court with men of reputation and understanding, who fear God, hate covetousness, and love His law.

Chief Justice Roy Moore was such a man. In this lecture, Chief Justice Roy Moore will speak from his experience about the essential relationship between Christianity and the judiciary. He will explain how the powers of the judiciary have been expanded beyond those expressly granted in the United States Constitution. Moreover, he will describe why Christian men who stand on the Word of God with integrity can never fail.

Lecture Outline

1. **The Turning of America Away from God**

   A. The faith of George Washington

   B. One nation under God

   C. Saint Paul's Church

2. **The First Amendment of the United States Constitution**

   A. The false interpretation of the First Amendment has been the source of abuses

   B.   A national day of prayer and fasting was called

3. **The French Revolution as a War Against Christianity**

   A. The public worship of God was outlawed

   B.   A new calendar was organized to reject the Christian chronology

   C. Christian holidays were abolished

4. **The Battle for the Ten Commandments**

   A. American officials have declared war on the acknowledgment of God

   B. Chief Justice Roy Moore was removed from office by men who mirrored the spirit of anarchy demonstrated during the French Revolution and not the God fearing men of America's own founding.

   C. Every State Constitution acknowledges God

5. **The Central Modern Issue is Acknowledging the Sovereignty of God**

6. **The Tale of Two Cities**

   A. The French Revolution is juxtaposed to America's founding

    B.   Declaring themselves to be wise those who deny God become fools

7. The Rejection of God in the American Judicial System

    A.   Modern judges twist the original meaning to reach a desired result

    B.   The result of judicial rulings not founded on the morality of Scripture has been devastating

    C.   When there are no standards, judges will make up standards as they go

8. The Devastation of Crooked Precedent

    A.   Judges often uphold wrongs because those wrongs are a matter of precedent

    B.   Precedent is important, but must be established on the Law of God

Questions

1.   What was the first official act of George Washington as U.S. President?

_____

_____

_____

2.   Who does the First Amendment of the United States Constitution limit?

_____

_____

_____

3.   What was the first act of Congress after the final language of the First Amendment was drafted?

_____

_____

_____

4. How many people did the French Government under the influence of the "Enlightenment" murder during the French revolution?

_____

_____

_____

5. Why was Chief Justice Roy Moore removed from office?

_____

_____

_____

6. What effect did the "Enlightenment" have on the modern political system?

_____

_____

_____

7. Why is the sovereignty of God a central issue in matters of law and among the judiciary?

_____

_____

_____

8. What are the two examples that Chief Justice Moore provides as resulting from the abandonment of God's law in the judiciary?

_____

_____

_____

9. What is the consequence of Christians who fail to recognize that morality comes from God?

_____

_____

_____

10. How does the use of international law undermine the authority of the United States Constitution?

_____

_____

_____

Selected Reading

Henry de Bracton, in his *On the Laws and Customs of England*, speaks on the importance of appointing judges:

> *"Let no one, unwise and unlearned, presume to ascend the seat of judgment, which is like unto the throne of God, lest for light he bring darkness and for darkness light, and, with unskillful hand, even as a madman, he put the innocent to the sword and set free the guilty, and lest he fall from on high, as from the throne of God, in attempting to fly before he has wings. And though one is fit to judge and to be made a judge, let each one take care for himself lest, by judging perversely and against the laws, because of prayer or price, for the advantage of a temporary and insignificant gain, he dare to bring upon himself sorrow and lamentation everlasting, and lest in the day of the wrath of the Lord he feel the vengeance of Him who said, 'Vengeance is mine, I will repay, on that day when kings and princes of the earth shall weep and bewail when they behold the Son of Man, because of fear of his torments, where gold and silver will be of no avail to set them free.*
>
> *Who shall not fear that trial, where the Lord shall be the accuser, the advocate and the judge? From his sentence there is no appeal, for the Father has committed all judgment to the Son; he shuts and there is none to open; he opens and there is none to shut. O how strict shall that judgment be, where we shall give account not only of our acts but*

even of every idle word that men utter. Who can escape his impending wrath? For the Son of Man shall send His angels and they shall gather out of His kingdom all things that offend and them that do iniquity and bind them into bundles to be burnt, and shall cast them into the fiery furnace, where there will be wailing and gnashing of teeth, groans and screams, outcries, lamentation and torment, roaring and shouting, fear and trembling, sorrow and suffering, fire and stench, doubt and anxiety, violence and cruelty, ruin and poverty, distress and dejection, oblivion and confusion, tortures and woundings, troubles and terrors, hunger and thirst, cold and heat, brimstone and burning fire for ever and ever. Therefore let each beware of that judgment where the judge is terribly strict, intolerably severe, offended beyond measure and vehemently angered, whose sentence none can commute, from whose prison there is no escape, whose punishments are without end, his tormentors horrible, who never grow weary, never pity, whom fear does not disturb, conscience condemn, thoughts reproach, and who may not flee. Hence, the blessed Augustine, 'O how far too great are my sins, wherefore when one has God as a rightful judge and his conscience as witness, let him fear nothing except his cause.'"

Definitions

Stare decisis: A legal doctrine by which judges will respect the precedent established by prior decisions.

Judicial Review: The theory rising out of *Marburry v. Madison*, which held that the Judicial Branch is the sole interpreter of the Constitutionality of acts of Congress and the Executive.

Writing Assignment

In 1965, the Supreme Court in *Griswold v. Connecticut* considered a law in the State of Connecticut, which had outlawed the trafficking of contraceptives. Desiring to rule against the law, but not having the constitutional grounds to do so, the court found that the law was invalid under the "penumbras and emanations" of the Constitution. This case laid the groundwork for future cases such as *Roe v. Wade*, which stated a woman had the right to kill her child, and *Lawrence v. Texas* which ruled that there was a constitutional right to practice homosexuality. Write a 500-word essay describing the dangers of setting bad precedent. Discuss the precedents that Justice Roy Moore set by acting with integrity in the face of oppressive government.

Recommendations for Further Study

So Help Me God, by Justice Roy Moore

Government by Judiciary, By Raoul Berger

How to Dethrone the Imperial Judiciary, by Edwin Vieira

Blackstone Commentaries on the Common Law of England, by Sir William Blackstone

Unit Six–Lesson 3
Canon Law and Ecclesiastical Courts

Introduction

The Canon Law and ecclesiastical courts have always been an important aspect of the church since its beginning. From the earliest stages of the church, we discover that the Jerusalem Council had the binding authority to hear and decide questions of orthodoxy[40] and to settle disputes between religious factions in the church[41]. From Paul we discover that the churches also had ecclesiastical courts that had the binding authority to settle civil conflict that arose between brethren.[42] This system of government was nothing new to the Jewish believers who had lived under the civil rule of Roman authority, but had retained the right to interpret and enforce the Law of God in the synagogues, even in nations and cities located outside of Israel.[43] This distinction between Civil Law and Canon Law, each with its own judicial system, was built into the early church government from the beginning.

The authority of the civil magistrate is enforced by the power of the sword, to coerce justice by force and execute evildoers for capital crimes. The authority of the ecclesiastical court is enforced by the power of the keys, to coerce by alienation from the church and the sacraments. Although, the early church regarded the books of the New Testament as Scripture, the Canon was not finalized and many books of the New Testament were not universally accessible. This led the early Church to heavily rely on the Old Testament. As Christianity gained dominance over western civilization these two judicial systems continued separate and distinct, but the Law of God was considered as binding over both.

This establishment of a two-court system continued in early Christian Roman Law and quickly spread throughout the Kingdoms of Europe. At times throughout western history, these two separate powers become confused as civil and ecclesiastical authorities sometimes attempted to dominate the jurisdiction of the other. However, this two-court system was preserved throughout the history of the western legal tradition.

This two-court system began to break down during the enlightenment, although there are traces of it in some places and among a few denominations. First, ecclesiastical courts began to break down as Churches abandoned the law of God. Enlightenment philosophy tended to complement theologies that held the idea that the law of God was only relevant to "spiritual matters" of "personal salvation" which were to be freely determined on the basis of the private choice of the individual. Second, churches increasingly held themselves out as independent from the larger body of Christ, which severed the solidarity enjoyed by ecclesiastical courts for more than two millennia. This also allowed individuals who did not like the determination of one church to simply apply themselves to the membership of another church. Thirdly, a huge number of the population denied the faith and/or have become theological liberals who deny the authority of Scripture. This replaced a time when a non-Christian who desired to prosper in a Christian society still placed themselves under the Church's authority, because Christians only trusted to do business with those who could be held accountable for their civil wrongs. Fourthly, the authority of the church to bind in heaven what is bound on earth and the power to hand unrepentant members over to the torment of Satan, has been largely ignored by church leaders and members alike. Finally, this two-court system has dissipated because many churches are unwilling to practice church discipline in a biblical manner. Even among those churches that do practice church discipline, many ministers feel qualified only to speak to matters of gross immoral behavior and not to issues of civil and social injustice.

In this lecture, Dr. Joseph Morecraft will expound on the biblical authority of the church. He will discuss the biblical structure for church government and will speak of the vital importance of the practice of church discipline in the church. Finally, he will talk about why ecclesiastical courts are important to the vitality of a nation and why Christian statesmen should dedicate themselves fully to the strengthening and defense of the Church of Jesus Christ.

Lecture Outline

1. The Keys of Ecclesiastical Authority

    A. Matthew 16:15-19

    B. Matthew 18:18-20

2. Jesus is the Head of the Church

    A. The word of Christ is Law

    B. The Scripture the rule of faith

3. Five Foundational Principles of Church Government

    A. The church elects its own officers (Acts 14:23)

    B. Church elders have equality of authority (Acts 20:17, 28)

    C. Local churches are to have a plurality of elders

    D. Ordination to office is the act of the Presbytery (1 Timothy 4:14)

    E. Church members have the right to appeal to the Presbytery (Acts 15)

4. The Nature and Extent of the Church's Authority

    A. The source of church authority is Christ, not the people

    B. The standard of church authority: The entire Word of God

    C. The nature of this authority is ministerial and not legislative

5. The Jurisdiction of Church Authority

    A. Jurisdiction over matters of doctrine

    B. Jurisdiction over matters of worship

    C. Jurisdiction in matters relating to church discipline

6. The Maintenance of the Doctrine and Life of the Church

    A. A credible profession of faith

    B. The practice of church discipline

        i.   Preventative discipline

        ii. Restorative discipline

        iii. Corrective discipline

C. The preaching of the Word of God

7. The Procedure of Church Discipline

A. The offended person is to approach the offender

B. The offended takes a witness to approach an offender

C. The offended approaches the elders

D. An unrepentant offender is to be excluded from the church in hopes of restoration

8. The Separation of Church and State

A. Christ is the head of both Church and State

B. The State is a ministry of justice

C. The Church is a ministry of grace

D. Israel observed a separation of Church and State

9. The Duty of the State Toward the Church

A. The State is the civil protector of the Church

10. The Duty of the Church Toward the State

A. The Church has a prophetic duty to call the State to repentance

B. The Church is to have a sanctifying influence on the State

11. The Relation of Church Courts to Civil Courts

A. The Church is an independent and limited jurisdiction of influence

B. The State is also an independent and limited jurisdiction of influence

12. The Christian Use of the Civil Courts

A. Christians should not go to court when it brings reproach to the name of Christ

B. Christians should exhaust all other remedies

C. Christians must put aside revenge and retaliation

D. Christians must be willing to suffer injury for the glory of God

E. An improper lust for possession should not divide brethren

F. The Christian must know how to properly apply the Law of God

Questions

1. In Scripture, what are keys symbolic of?

    _____

    _____

    _____

2. In Acts 14:23, what does the word "appoint" mean in the Greek language?

    _____

    _____

    _____

3. What is the standard by which the local church should establish and carry out its form of church government?

    _____

    _____

    _____

4. What is the difference between an elder and a bishop?

    _____

    _____

    _____

5. What is a presbytery according to the Scripture?

    _____

    _____

    _____

6. How has the Church been the guardian of truth to the world?

_____

_____

_____

7. What does the Regulative Principle of Worship mean?

_____

_____

_____

8. What is the one requirement that Scripture provides for membership in the Church?

_____

_____

_____

9. Who is involved in the work of counseling and church discipline?

_____

_____

_____

10. What is the purpose of civil courts?

_____

_____

_____

Further Reading

Patrick Henry, in his famous speech, which ends with the much quoted "Give me liberty or give me death," speaks of God as the source of that liberty:

> *"They tell us, sir, that we are weak; unable to cope with so formidable an adversary. But when shall we be stronger? Will it be the next week, or the next year? Will it be when we are totally disarmed, and when a British guard shall be stationed in every house? Shall we gather strength by irresolution and inaction? Shall we acquire the means of effectual resistance, by lying supinely on our backs, and hugging the delusive phantom of hope, until our enemies shall have bound us hand and foot? Sir, we are not weak if we make a proper use of those means which the God of nature hath placed in our power. Three millions of people, armed in the holy cause of liberty, and in such a country as that which we possess, are invincible by any force which our enemy can send against us. Besides, sir, we shall not fight our battles alone. There is a just God who presides over the destinies of nations; and who will raise up friends to fight our battles for us. The battle, sir, is not to the strong alone; it is to the vigilant, the active, the brave. Besides, sir, we have no election. If we were base enough to desire it, it is now too late to retire from the contest. There is no retreat but in submission and slavery! Our chains are forged! Their clanking may be heard on the plains of Boston! The war is inevitable and let it come! I repeat it, sir, let it come.*
>
> *It is in vain, sir, to extenuate the matter. Gentlemen may cry, Peace, Peace but there is no peace. The war is actually begun! The next gale that sweeps from the north will bring to our ears the clash of resounding arms! Our brethren are already in the field! Why stand we here idle? What is it that gentlemen wish? What would they have? Is life so dear, or peace so sweet, as to be purchased at the price of chains and slavery? Forbid it, Almighty God! I know not what course others may take; but as for me, give me liberty or give me death!"*

Definitions

Canon Law: Law based on the Scripture and counsels of the Church

Excommunication: The act of church discipline in which an unrepentant offender is cut off from the Lord's table and from the fellowship of the saints.

Ecclesiastical Courts: A judicial system established in Christian churches that hear disputes over which the church has jurisdiction.

Writing Assignment

Many churches today have abandoned the scriptural practice of church discipline, claiming it to be unloving and foreign to the practices of the modern church. This has lead to a great loss of purity in the church. It also has diminished the role of the church in the community. Write a 500-word essay that surveys the biblical model for church discipline. Using what you have learned in this lesson, include a discussion regarding the purpose of church discipline and why it is an important function of the church.

Recommendations for Further Study

The Apostolic Church, Which Is It?, by Thomas Witherow

The Handbook of Church Discipline, by Jay A. Adams

The Church of Christ, by James Bannerman

Unit Seven

Unit Seven–Lesson 1
The Legislative Branch

Introduction

The Constitution of the United States vests all legislative powers in the Congress of the United States. The Congress of the United States is the most powerful branch of government. It is the first branch of government mentioned in the Constitution and in many ways is the centerpiece of American Republicanism. The Congress is divided into two houses. Originally, the Senate was made up of senators who had been appointed by their state legislators to represent the interest of the states in Congress and to safeguard federalism. States were to be represented equally in the Senate, each state having two senators, regardless of population. The House of Representatives was intended to be the people's house since, unlike the president, the Senate, and the Supreme Court Justices, representatives were elected by popular election based on local populations.

The Congress of the United States has vast powers, but these are by no means unlimited. Its ability to legislate is limited to a specific number of areas.

First, Congress has the power over the federal purse. This is commonly known as the taxing and spending powers. Congress may raise taxes, duties, imposes, and excises and allocate them for a limited number of purposes. Congress also has the authority to barrow money on the credit of the United States.

Second, Congress has the authority to maintain the military of the United States. Congress may raise armies, declare war, and pass laws in order to provide for the common defense. However, while Congress has the sole authority to declare war, the president is the commander and chief of the military. Most modern wars are unconstitutional since they have not been declared by Congress. Moreover, any appropriation made for rising and supporting armies is limited to the term of two years.

Third, Congress has the power to regulate interstate commerce between the states. This power has been unconstitutional expanded to also include intrastate commerce and to regulate non-commercial activities that remotely effect commerce. This expansion of power has been used by Congress as a virtual plenary power to regulate areas previously unreachable by federal power.

Fourth, Congress has the authority to regulate immigration and naturalization. Congress also has the authority to exclusively regulate special areas of law such as maritime law, bankruptcy, copyright, and patent law.

Fifth, Congress has the sole authority to coin money and fix standards for weights and measures. As has been discussed in previous lessons this is an area of authority over which Congress has unconstitutional abdicated to private banks.

Sixth, Congress has the authority to establish and regulate a post office.

Seven, Congress has the authority to establish inferior Federal Court under the Supreme Court and to regulate the Supreme Court's appellate jurisdiction.

Eight, Congress has the authority to regulate the District of Columbia and all federal lands.

Nine, Congress has the authority to engage in foreign policy. This power is shared with the President of the United States.

Ten, Congress has the authority to enforce the 13th, 14th, and 15th amendments.

All acts of Congress must fall into one of these categories or it is an unconstitutional expansion of congressional power. The legal effect of the Constitution against such laws renders these laws null and void. The Christian statesman must be aware of the proper function and limits on Congressional power.

In this lecture, Doug Phillips will talk about the nature of law and the continuing relevance of God's Law on legislators today. He will discuss why all legislatures are limited in their ability to "make law." Finally, he will emphasize that all legislative authority is ultimately rooted in God's establishment civil government as recorded in the book of Genesis.

Lecture Outline

1. The Battle in Every Area of Life: What Standard Will Govern?

    A. The autonomous reason of man?

    B. The holy Word of God?

2. Reformation Position: The Authority of the Word of God for All of Life

3. Three Tiers of God's Law

    A. The two greatest commandments (Matthew 22:37-40)

    B. The ten commandments

    C. Case laws

4. Characteristics of the Moral Law of God

    A. Always existed

    B. Based on the holy, unchanging character of God

    C. Unchangeable

5. The Importance of Genesis in Understanding Law

    A. All of the basic principle of law are established in the first 11 chapters of Genesis

    B. Examples of different principles found in Genesis

6. Genesis' Law Principles

    A. The jurisdiction of all authority

    B. The equality of all men

    C. The establishment of covenants

    D. Criminal justice, judicial authority

    E. The principles of war and arms

7. Common Law

    A. Grounded in the doctrine of the Creator

B. The source of law is revealed by the Creator not the creation

8. The Principles Guiding the Common Law Found in:

A. The dominion charter

B. The Sabbath

C. The Atonement

D. The tree of life

E. Marriage

9. The Ten Commandments in the Garden of Eden

C. Worship and obey God only-not the snake

D. Do not commit idolatry for the tree

E. Do not take the Lord's name in vain

F. Keep the Sabbath

G. Honor your father (and the heavenly Father)

H. Do not murder

I. Do not commit adultery

J. Do not steal

K. Do not lie

L. Do not covet

10. Areas in Common Law

A. Criminal Law

B. Tort Law

C. Evidence Law

D. Real and Personal Property Law

E. Contract Law

11. God Given Law

A. Revealed law: special revelation

1. Appearances of God

2. Prophecies

3. Miracles

    B. General revelation

12. William Blackstone on the Sufficiency of Scriptures

13. False Theories

    A. "Christ has freed us from the necessity of law"

    B. "There is tension between grace and law"

    C. "To believe in the relevance of the law is to believe that the law saves"

14. The Theonomic Pyramid

    A. The two greatest commandments

    B. The ten commandments

    C. The case laws

15. Observations of the Three-Tiered Approach

    F. The law asserts principles

    G. The law cities cases to develop the implications of these principles

    H. The law has as its purpose and direction the restitution of God's order

16. Examples of How the Theonomic Pyramid (The Three Tiers) Work in Different Cases

Questions

1. What is the reformation position regarding the governing of all of life?

_____

_____

_____

2. What are the three tiers of God's law?

_____

_____

_____

3. What are some characteristics of the moral law of God?

_____

_____

_____

4. What are some law principles found in Genesis?

_____

_____

_____

5. What does equality of all men mean?

_____

_____

_____

6. What are some of the principles of the Ten Commandments found in the Garden of Eden?

_____

_____

_____

7. What do the case laws illustrate?

_____

_____

_____

8. What are some areas of law found in the Common Law?

_____

_____

_____

9. What are some false theories regarding the law of God?

_____

_____

_____

10. What is the purpose and direction of the law?

_____

_____

_____

Selected Reading

Sir William Blackstone, in his *Commentaries on the Laws of England*, writes about the general nature of law:

> "This then is the general signification of law, a rule of action dictated
> by some superior being: and, in those creatures that have neither the
> power to think, nor to will, such laws must be invariably obeyed, so
> long as the creature itself subsists, for its existence depends on that
> obedience. But laws, in their more confined sense, and in which it is
> our present business to consider them, denote the rules, not of action in

general, but of human action or conduct: that is, the precepts by which man, the noblest of all sublunary beings, a creature endowed with both reason and freewill, is commanded to make use of those faculties in the general regulation of his behavior.

Man, considered as a creature, must necessarily be subject to the laws of his creator, for he is entirely a dependent being. A being, independent of any other, has no rule to pursue, but such as he prescribes to himself; but a state of dependence will inevitably oblige the inferior to take the will of him, on whom he depends, as the rule of his conduct: not indeed in every particular, but in all those points wherein his dependence consists. This principle therefore has more or less extent and effect, in proportion as the superiority of the one and the dependence of the other is greater or less, absolute or limited. And consequently, as man depends absolutely upon his maker for every thing, it is necessary that he should in all points conform to his maker's will.

This will of his maker is called the law of nature. For as God, when he created matter, and endued it with a principle of mobility, established certain rules for the perpetual direction of that motion; so, when he created man, and endued him with freewill to conduct himself in all parts of life, he laid down certain immutable laws of human nature, whereby that freewill is in some degree regulated and restrained, and gave him also the faculty of reason to discover the purport of those laws.

Considering the creator only as a being of infinite power, he was able unquestionably to have prescribed whatever laws he pleased to his creature, man, however unjust or severe. But as he is also a being of infinite wisdom, he has laid down only such laws as were founded in those relations of justice, that existed in the nature of things antecedent to any positive precept. These are the eternal, immutable laws of good and evil, to which the creator himself in all his dispensations conforms; and which he has enabled human reason to discover, so far as they are necessary for the conduct of human actions. Such among others are these principles: that we should live honestly, should hurt nobody, and should render to every one his due; to which three general precepts Justinian has reduced the whole doctrine of law."

Definitions

Theonomy: The belief that God's law is binding on the civil government.

General revelation: Revelation that is innate in all men flowing from nature and grace.

Special revelation: Revelation that is given to specific individuals at specific times issuing from the spirit of God.

Writing Assignment

A television show once hosted a panel of individuals, one of whom was an influential figure in the Christian community on public policy issues. When asked whether he believed that Americans should draw from the Law of God as a source of law, the Christian fumbled over his words and finally said no. Instead, he said he thought the Ancient Code of Hammurabi should be influencing the laws in the United States. Attempting to appear wise in the sight of unbelievers, he became a fool. Write a 500-word essay about the importance of observing the Law of God today. Include a discussion of the importance of Christians to firmly stand unashamed on the Law of God.

Recommendations for Further Study

The Institutes of Biblical Law, by R.J. Rushdoony

Commentaries on the Laws of England, by William Blackstone

A Forgotten Giant of the Reformation, by Jean-Marc Berthoud

Institutes of the Christian Religion, by John Calvin

Theonomy in Christian Ethics, by Greg Bahnsen

Unit Seven–Lesson 2
Christianity and the Common Law

Introduction

The American legal system did not begin anew after the ratification of the Constitution. Rather a significant portion of the American legal system represents a continuance of the English Common Law. Modern laws of contract, tort, criminal law, evidence, civil procedure, property, wills, trusts, and future interests all largely consist of concepts deeply rooted in the English Common Law. The English Common Law is a masterwork of the Christian legal tradition, consisting of constitutions, bills of rights, legislation, and case law, which slowly developed for well over a millennia.

The Common Law of England began with the birth of England as a united nation and it is rooted in the legislation of England's first king, Alfred the Great. Alfred came to power during perilous times. The British Isles were broken up into a number of Anglo-Saxon kingdoms, each of which were relentlessly plundered and scattered by Viking Raiders. During that time, Anglo-Saxon churches served as banks, libraries, and schools, as well as being houses of worship. This made them the particular target of the plundering Danes. The destruction of these churches caused a sharp increase of illiteracy, poverty, and hardship among the Anglo-Saxon people.

Alfred united England by raising an army and navy that was able to withstand the Danish forces. As the Danes were beaten back, Alfred restored the churches, rebuilt cities, and set up watch posts for the protection and preservation of Anglo-Saxon communities. Alfred's commitment to spread the Gospel among his subjects was as strong as his desire to defeat the Danes. Alfred translated several important books into the common tongue and wrote books for common instruction. These include portions of the Bible and Bede's *Church History*, so that the Anglo-Saxon people would understand their national history. Alfred also originated the Anglo-Saxon chronicles as a means of instructing future generations. Central to the government of the new English kingdom under Alfred, were the laws he enacted, commonly called the *Dooms of Alfred the Great*. Alfred understood that civil authority was derived from the Supreme Governor of the universe. Alfred's Dooms contained the full text of the Ten Commandments, case laws from Exodus, selections from the Sermon on the Mount, and the rulings of the Jerusalem council recorded in the Acts of the Apostles.

Moreover, the *Dooms of Alfred* laid the very foundation for benefits that Americans enjoy today, such as limited government, and equality under the law. Alfred wrote, "Doom very evenly! Do not doom one doom to the rich; another to the poor! Nor doom one doom to your friend; another to your foe." The *Dooms of Alfred* would be expanded to lay the foundations of the English Common Law, which is the foundation of the legal system in America today. It would establish a legacy which eventually lead to the *Magna Charta* and the English Bill of Rights, the precursors to the Constitution of the United States.

The American legal system is permeated with the influence of Christianity; being established on the Law of God. There is not a day that goes by in the average courtroom in which, in some manner, the Law of God is not introduced as a source of order and justice. Legal hallmarks of American government such as limited government, local self-government, and equality under the law, have their foundations in the development of an intrinsically Christian view of law ad public policy. In this lecture, Doug Phillips will discuss the importance of the Common Law to the American legal system. He will chart the history of the Common Law to the time of the Hebrew republic and demonstrate how the history of the Common Law proves that unless the Lord builds the house, they labor in vain who build it.

Lecture Outline

1. John Witherspoon

   A. Lawyers and magistrates are ministers of God; Romans 13

   B. John Adams on Witherspoon "A true son of liberty he was. But first he was a son of the Cross"

   C. Educator, clergyman, and president of Princeton's College

   D. Trained a generation of leaders

2. Leopold and Loeb Murder Trial: Attorney Clarence Darrow

   A. The most important trial of the 21st Century

   B. The product of evolutionary thinking

3. Faith: Hebrews 11:1-2

   A. All men have faith

   B. Faith is objective or irrational

   C. Christianity, the only rational faith

4. Does a Fish Knows It is Wet?

   A. The Desert Island Challenge

5. By What Standard?

   A. He who defines wins

   B. 1 Timothy 1:8

   C. The answer is God's Word

6. What is Law?

   A. "A rule of action dictated by a superior being.": Sir William Blackstone

7. Types of Law:

   A. Positive Law: men create law out of nothing and it becomes truth by majority action

   B. Natural Law

   C. Evolutionary Law

8. Epistemology

A. Definition: "The study of the nature, sources, and limits of human knowledge."

9. Presupposition

A. Definition: "An elementary assumption. A basic commitment. A foundational perspective in which experiences and facts are interpreted."

10. Total Sovereignty is Inescapable; Either

A. Man is sovereign

B. The State is sovereign

C. God is sovereign

11. God's Judgment for Four Crimes

A. Idolatrous false worship

B. Child sacrifice

C. Moral perversion

D. Effeminacy and abdication by men

12. The Mixed Response of the "Church"—Many:

A. Embraced political pluralism

B. Persecuted, mocked and ridiculed those standing for Christ

C. Placed partisan goals above principled actions

13. Will God Restore Our Judges?

A. Isaiah 1:26

14. John Winthrop

A. *A Model of Christian Charity*

B. What is government?

C. Types of government: self government, family, church, and state government

15. The Christian View of Reality, Knowledge, and Facts

    A. The Bible is "sourcebook" for all truth

    B. God's knowledge is original, comprehensive and creative

    C. All knowledge and wisdom are deposited in Christ; God's Word had final authority

16. Foundational Principles

    A. The Bible as a self-authenticating witness

    B. The unchanging character and attributes of a sovereign God

    C. The continuing validity of the law of God

    D. The superiority of special revelation over general revelation

    E. The Lordship of Christ

    F. The priesthood of the believer

    G. The sufficiency and perspicuity of Scripture

    H. The religious nature of thought

    I. The myth of neutrality

17. Essential Questions for Christian Lawyers and Leaders

    A. Can man legislate morality?

    B. By what standard will we govern?

    C. Does this standard evolve or change?

18. Pop Quiz

19. What Isn't Meant by a Christian America

20. What Is Meant by a Christian America

21. Ten Evidences That America is a Christian Commonwealth

    A. The Settlement

    B. Colonial charters

    C. State constitutions

    D. Religious oaths

E. Biblical Law and Common Law

F. Colonial education

G. Testimony of the founders

H. Rulings and declarations

I. Demographics and other testimonies

J. The Declaration and Constitution

22. The Constitution as a Christian Document

A. The subscription clause

B. The Constitution as a Christian civil covenant

C. National birthday based on Declaration of Independence. Constitution is not a new covenant, but the creation of "a more perfect union" of the covenant of 1776

D. Expressly relied on the Declaration as the founding document, and the Declaration is predicated and concluded on an acknowledgement of the God of the Bible

E. Adopted the Christian calendar

F. Adopted the Common Law

G. The signing of the treaty with Great Britain ending the war for Independence

23. Common Law Part of the Document

24. Holy Trinity Versus United States Case

25. The First Amendment

A. Only applied to the Federal Government

B. Prevented the Federal Government from usurping state rights and individual liberties by discriminating between Christian denominations

C. Prevented the Federal Government from restricting the right of the states to establish state churches and discriminate in favor of denominational Christianity

Questions

1. What does the case of Leopold and Loeb encompass?

_____

_____

_____

2. What is the most important question that defines all the other ones?

_____

_____

_____

3. What is positive law?

_____

_____

_____

4. What does it mean to be "epistemologically self-conscious"?

_____

_____

_____

5. What is a presupposition?

_____

_____

_____

6. What are the four crimes that invoke God's judgment?

_____

_____

_____

7. What sermon by John Winthrop influenced the first colonies ?

_____

_____

_____

8. According to William Blackstone what is law ?

_____

_____

_____

9. According to Van Til what is the Bible?

_____

_____

_____

10. What is the reason for the First Amendment?

_____

_____

_____

Selected Reading

The Westminster Confession of Faith concerning the Civil Magistrate:

> *"I. God, the supreme Lord and King of all the world, has ordained civil magistrates, to be, under Him, over the people, for His own glory, and the public good: and, to this end, has armed them with the power of the sword, for the defense and encouragement of them that are good, and for the punishment of evil doers.*
>
> *II. It is lawful for Christians to accept and execute the office of a magistrate, when called thereunto: in the managing whereof, as they ought especially to maintain piety, justice, and peace, according to the wholesome laws of each commonwealth; so, for that end, they may lawfully, now under the New Testament, wage war, upon just and necessary occasion.*
>
> *III. Civil magistrates may not assume to themselves the administration of the Word and sacraments; or the power of the keys of the kingdom of heaven; yet he has authority, and it is his duty, to take order that unity and peace be preserved in the Church, that the truth of God be kept pure and entire, that all blasphemies and heresies be suppressed, all corruptions and abuses in worship and discipline prevented or reformed, and all the ordinances of God duly settled, administrated, and observed. For the better effecting whereof, he has power to call synods, to be present at them and to provide that whatsoever is transacted in them be according to the mind of God.*
>
> *IV. It is the duty of people to pray for magistrates, to honor their persons, to pay them tribute or other dues, to obey their lawful commands, and to be subject to their authority, for conscience' sake. Infidelity, or difference in religion, does not make void the magistrates' just and legal authority, nor free the people from their due obedience to them: from which ecclesiastical persons are not exempted, much less has the Pope any power and jurisdiction over them in their dominions, or over any of their people; and, least of all, to deprive them of their dominions, or lives, if he shall judge them to be heretics, or upon any other pretense whatsoever."*

Definitions

Presupposition: An elementary assumption, a basic faith commitment, a foundational perspective in which experiences and facts are interpreted.

Perspicuity of Scripture: Scripture's ability to communicate with clarity.

Subscription Clause: predicates an act on an oath to Jesus Christ by the delegates to the Constitution; links the Constitution to the God of the Bible and the Christian foundation of the nation.

Writing Assignment

The Church of Jesus Christ has had a profound effect on the Western legal system to the point that to eradicate Christianity from Western law is to altogether do away with Western law. Since the Scriptures teach a separation of church and state, many have theorized about how to allow the Church to play an advisory role in the affairs of the state without becoming excessively entangled in the State's jurisdiction. In Calvin's Geneva they formed what are called consistories, a body composed of churchmen and civil rulers, to allow the Church and the State to confer with one another without stepping into the other's jurisdiction. Write a 500-word essay on the importance of the influence of the Church on the State.

Recommendations for Further Study

Of Plymouth Plantation, by William Bradford

American Political Writing During the Founding, by Charles S. Hyneman

The American Republic: Primary Sources, by Bruce Frohnen

The Constitutional Documents of the Puritan Revolution, 1625-1660, by Samuel Rawson Gardiner

Unit Seven–Lesson 3
Citizens of the Kingdom of God

Introduction

Standing before Pontius Pilate Jesus said, "My kingdom is not of this world: if my kingdom were of this world, then would my servants fight, that I should not be delivered to the Jews: but now is my kingdom not from hence."[44] An understanding of what Jesus was communicating is important to how a Christian is to understand the law of nations. Many Christians popularly quote this verse as if to agree with the declarations of the Jews in the following chapter, "We have not king but Caesar."[45] In other words, many Christians believe the idea that Christ's kingdom is not of this world, that He is only concerned with heavenly things and He is not concerned with matters of local civil government. According to them, it is not Christ who reigns supreme over this earthly civil realm, but Caesar.

However, the message that Christ was communicating was not one of abdication from the earthly realm, but one of absolute superiority over the earthly realm. Christ is the King of kings and Lord of lords, Whose Kingdom cannot be pulled down by the kingdoms of this earth. Moreover, Christ was not saying that

His servants were incapable of fighting in this earthly realm, but rather that even in death His throne could not be disestablished, and so a fight was unnecessary. In effect, Jesus was communicating that he was a King transcendent to Caesar, and that the power of all the kingdoms of this world were powerless against Him.

Philippians 3:20 teaches Christians that their citizenship is in Heaven. This is also a verse that is often quoted and seldom understood. This is often cited with the intention of communicating that Christians should not concern themselves with the civil aspect of this life. On the contrary, Paul is making the point that because our citizenship is in heaven we have an obligation to walk as a testimony of that fact before unbelievers. Far from being temporarily misplaced in a world in which we do not belong, Christians are commanded to be an occupying force over a world that Christ has overcome.[46] Christians are also called to infiltrate every nation, teaching them to observe all things that Christ has commanded. Jesus described His disciples as salt, light, and a city on a hill. Christians are therefore to be a force of influence in the world around them.

Therefore, an understanding of the Law of Nations must begin with an understanding that Christ is the ruler of nations. As the ruler of nations, Christ demands that the earthly rulers make their reigns subservient to the divine glory. The sovereignty of Christ over all nations of this earth provides the biblical framework for a universal law which is binding on all nations, and establishes an ethical framework for how nations govern their internal and foreign affairs. Christians are compared to an occupying force to influence the world around them and to teach them how to submit to the authority of Christ.

In this lecture president of the Plymouth Rock Foundation, Paul Jehle, will introduce the framework for the Law of Nations. He will point out that the transformation of a nation begins in the transforming power of the Holy Spirit in the life of the believer. Moreover, he will explain that there is a parallel between out local relationship and how our nations approach each other. Finally, he will discuss the early history of the Law of Nations and how the theological presuppositions of the men who uncovered this important concept effected their treatment of the doctrine.

Lecture Outline

1. God Governs the Nations

    A. Psalm 22:27-28

2. Distinction Between Kingdoms and Nations

    A. The rule of Christ on the Earth

    B. Satan is the Enemy and he has a government

        i. Spirits

        ii. Principalities

        iii. Powers

        iv. Rulers of darkness

    C. Christ's Kingdom

        i. Christ converts individuals

        ii. Christ restores the family

        iii. Christ loves His Church

        iv. Nations

        v. Kingdom

3. Christians Are Engaged in a War

    A. The Light of the World

    B. Salt

    C. City on a Hill

4. The Law of Nations is an Outgrowth of the Kingdom

    A. A president may issue an executive order that seeks to implement policy enacted by Congress.

    B. Nations are extensions of families

    C. God opposes centralized governments

    D. God's people bring the covenant blessing to their nation.

5. How God Governs

    A. God governs by General Revelation

B. God governs through the conviction of sin

6. Biblical Covenants Are the Foundation for National Treaties

A. Sanctity

B. Sanction

C. Redemption

7. A Nation's Domestic Policy Guides its Foreign Policy

A. The source of law

B. The way of law

C. The oath of law

D. The priority of law

8. Deeper Covenant Establishes Broader Covenants

A. Covenant with God

B. Covenant of marriage

C. Church covenants

D. Town Charter and bylaws

E. Law of Nations

9. Hugo Grotius and the Law of Nations

A. Believed the Law of God only applied to consenting nations

10. Samuel Puffendorf

A. One Law of Nations Governs all Nations

B. All Nations are accountable to God.

C. Negative vs. Positive Law

11. Emerich de Vattel

12. Just War Doctrine

A. Just Cause

B. Just Conduct

Questions

1. Where should a Christian Statesman's loyalties be placed?

_____

_____

_____

2. How is the government of Satan structured?

_____

_____

_____

3. Where does God begin to structure His government?

_____

_____

_____

4. Where do nations come from?

_____

_____

_____

5. How do we know when a covenant is biblical?

_____

_____

_____

6. By what standard is our domestic and foreign policy governed?

_____

_____

_____

7. Who is the source of American Law?

_____

_____

_____

8. Which covenant produces the greatest consequences?

_____

_____

_____

9. Next to our covenant with God, what is the most important covenant?

_____

_____

_____

10. Who is the Father of the modern law of nations?

_____

_____

_____

Selected Reading

The Scottish Declaration of Arbroath, which declares the sovereignty of Scotland under Robert the Bruce is a forbearer to the United States Declaration of Independence:

"The Most Holy Fathers your predecessors gave careful heed to these things and bestowed many favors and numerous privileges on this same kingdom and people, as being the special charge of the Blessed Peter's brother. Thus our nation under their protection did indeed live in freedom and peace up to the time when that mighty prince the King of the English, Edward, the father of the one who reigns today, when our kingdom had no head and our people harbored no malice or treachery and were then unused to wars or invasions, came in the guise of a friend and ally to harass them as an enemy. The deeds of cruelty, massacre, violence, pillage, arson, imprisoning prelates, burning down monasteries, robbing and killing monks and nuns, and yet other outrages without number which he committed against our people, sparing neither age nor sex, religion nor rank, no one could describe nor fully imagine unless he had seen them with his own eyes.

But from these countless evils we have been set free, by the help of Him Who though He afflicts yet heals and restores, by our most tireless Prince, King and Lord, the Lord Robert. He, that his people and his heritage might be delivered out of the hands of our enemies, met toil and fatigue, hunger and peril, like another Maccabaeus or Joshua and bore them cheerfully. Him, too, divine providence, his right of succession according to our laws and customs which we shall maintain to the death, and the due consent and assent of us all have made our Prince and King. To him, as to the man by whom salvation has been wrought unto our people, we are bound both by law and by his merits that our freedom may be still maintained, and by him, come what may, we mean to stand. Yet if he should give up what he has begun, and agree to make us or our kingdom subject to the King of England or the English, we should exert ourselves at once to drive him out as our enemy and a subverter of his own rights and ours, and make some other man who was well able to defend us our King; for, as long as but a hundred of us remain alive, never will we on any conditions be brought under English rule. It is in truth not for glory, nor riches, nor honors that we are fighting, but for freedom—for that alone, which no honest man gives up but with life itself."

Definitions

Law of Nations: A set of laws that governs the manner in which foreign nations approach matters of foreign policy.

Sanction: A penalty for disobeying a law or rule of law.

Writing Assignment

In 532 A.D., a tax revolt broke out in Constantinople under the Emperor Justinian. Two leaders of the revolt escaped to the Church of Saint Lawrence, where they were granted sanctuary. The Emperor Justinian refused to order his guards into the church because this was considered the invasion of a kingdom over which he did not have jurisdiction, because churches fall within separate jurisdiction than that of the state. This practice developed into the legal doctrine of Sanctuary throughout Europe. The idea being that an enemy of the state was not necessarily an enemy of God. The citizen who became an enemy of the state because he chose to obey God rather than man could find refuge within the earthly embassies of the Kingdom of God: the Church. Consider churches today. Write a 500-word essay with regard to the manner in which churches should be approached as separated jurisdiction from that of the state. What kind of safeguards might be put in place in order to protect the Church against civil intruders?

Recommendations for Further Study

Liberty and Property, by Dan Ford

On God and Political Duty, by John Calvin, Editor, John T. McNeill

The Emergence of Liberty, by Douglas Kelly

A Common Law, by Rueben Alvarado

Unit Seven–Lesson 4
The Universal Applicability of Law

Introduction

When discussing the continued relevance of the Law of God over the nations it is often suggested that the civil Law of God was only given to Israel, and does not have continued relevance for nations today. This argument not only has several hermeneutical problems attached to it, but it inadvertently destroys the idea of a Christian Law of Nations over which God's Law is sovereign. These arguments would be similar to that of the Arminian legal theorist, Hugo Grotius, who posited that the Law of God was only relevant to those nations who adopted it. Yet, if the standard of ethics between nations is merely voluntary, then nations who wrong other nations without declaring the law of God as binding have a means of escape. A nation cannot be held accountable for violating a standard that it was not accountable to in the first place.

The Scriptures teach that God is sovereign over all whether they adopt His law or not. In Daniel 4:17, 35, the Word of God declares, "the most High rules in the kingdom of men, and gives it to whomsoever he will, and sets up over it the basest of men." "All the inhabitants of the earth are reputed as nothing: and he doeth according to his will in the army of heaven, and among the inhabitants of the earth: and none can stay his hand, or say unto him, what doest thou?" Here God is sovereign over all nations and His will is done without regard to the nations. Moreover, in I Chronicles 16:31, we find a command that all nations of earth recognize God as the sovereign over all the earth: "Let the heavens be glad, and let the earth rejoice: and let men say among the nations, The LORD reigns" In Psalms 47:7, we are told, "God is the King of all the earth."

Among nations that seek a secular "non-religious" state, believing themselves not to be bound by the law of God, we learn in Psalm 33:10, "The LORD bringeth the counsel of the heathen to naught: he makes the devices of the people of none effect." Moreover, we learn throughout Scripture that God is the righteous judge of all nations that violate His law.[45] This is an important perspective for the Christian statesman to maintain against the boasts of an unbelieving world that finds no room for the counsel of God in the political realm.

The Christian statesman must realize that the Law of God is universally applicable in all nations. These are three simple questions to ask:

(1) Is God sovereign over all of his creation? (Psalm 29:10, Matthew 28:18)

(2) Has He ordained the end from the beginning of the world? (Isaiah 14:24, 37:26; Ephesians 1:11; Peter 1:20)

(3) Does God fashion all the nations of the earth according to His will? (Daniel 4:35; Romans 9:20)

If a Christian is to answer in the affirmative to each of these questions, then the implications are far reaching. If God is sovereign over all men and nations then the Law of God is the highest law; and the highest duty of all men and nations is to obey and glorify God through it. If God has ordained the end from the beginning then it is a vain thing for a nation to resist this framework of sovereignty. And finally, if God fashions the nations of the earth according to His will, then it is only a matter of time that nations that disregard His will are chastised and made to conform to His will. Then the modern secularism that currently exists in the United States will not be able to resist the will of God, nor sustain itself in its vain imaginations.

In part two of this series on the Law of Nations, Paul Jehle will discuss the Law of Nations as it relates to America's early history and how the founder's understanding that God ruled the nations shaped the manner in which they approached foreign policy with other nations. Moreover, he will discuss how an observance of the Law of God deeply impacted the course of the nation early on, and how it is reflected in America's founding documents.

Lecture Outline

The Law of Nations and the Constitution

1. The Kingdom of God Transcends all Nations

A. Self-government is the self under government

2. The Constitutional Understanding of the Law of Nations

A. The Declaration of Independence claimed justification

B. Congress has jurisdiction over violations of the Law of Nations

3. The Law of Nations and Limited National Sovereignty

A. Hugo Grotius

B. Henry Weaten

C. John Foster

D. James Wilson

E. William Wolleston

F. Alexander Hamilton

4. There is No Interdependence on Another Nation

A. George Washington: The Law of Beneficence

5. No Intermeddling

A. Alexander Hamilton

B. Monroe Doctrine

6. Interposition

7. Enumerated Powers

A. Congress

B. Executive

C. Judicial

8. The Supremacy of the Constitution

    A. Treaties and Federalist #64.

9. War of 1812

    A. The Executive could not declare war.

10. Annexation of Texas

Questions

1.   What does self-government imply?

_____

_____

_____

2.   What authority does the Declaration of Independence appeal to for justification?

_____

_____

_____

3.   What universal principle applied to the signing of treaties?

_____

_____

_____

4.   What did James Wilson mean when he said that the law of nations was of the people?

_____

_____

_____

5. Should America intervene in the internal problems of other nations?

_____

_____

_____

6. What was the response of the United States toward nations in South America who were fighting for their independence?

_____

_____

_____

7. What is the Monroe Doctrine?

_____

_____

_____

8. Why did the Executive approach Congress prior to the War of 1812?

_____

_____

_____

9. Which branch of government has been vested with the majority of the foreign policy powers?

_____

_____

_____

10. What did President James Polk feel the need to prove when Texas was annexed into the United States?

_____

_____

_____

Selected Reading

On December 2, 1823, President James Monroe delivered his seventh annual address to Congress in which he laid an American framework for Foreign Policy that later became known as The Monroe Doctrine:

> *"The Government of the United States has been desirous by this friendly proceeding of manifesting the great value which they have invariably attached to the friendship of the Emperor and their solicitude to cultivate the best understanding with his Government. In the discussions to which this interest has given rise and in the arrangements by which they may terminate the occasion has been judged proper for asserting, as a principle in which the rights and interests of the United States are involved, that the American continents, by the free and independent condition which they have assumed and maintain, are henceforth not to be considered as subjects for future colonization by any European powers...*
>
> *Of events in that quarter of the globe, with which we have so much intercourse and from which we derive our origin, we have always been anxious and interested spectators. The citizens of the United States cherish sentiments the most friendly in favor of the liberty and happiness of their fellow-men on that side of the Atlantic. In the wars of the European powers in matters relating to themselves we have never taken any part, nor does it comport with our policy to do so. It is only when our rights are invaded or seriously menaced that we resent injuries or make preparation for our defense....*
>
> *With the existing colonies or dependencies of any European power we have not interfered and shall not interfere. But with the Governments who have declared their independence and maintain it, and whose independence we have, on great consideration and on just principles, acknowledged, we could not view any interposition for the purpose of oppressing them, or controlling in any other manner their destiny, by any European power in any other light than as the*

manifestation of an unfriendly disposition toward the United States.

It is impossible that the allied powers should extend their political system to any portion of either continent without endangering our peace and happiness; nor can anyone believe that our southern brethren, if left to themselves, would adopt it of their own accord. It is equally impossible, therefore, that we should behold such interposition in any form with indifference. If we look to the comparative strength and resources of Spain and those new Governments, and their distance from each other, it must be obvious that she can never subdue them. It is still the true policy of the United States to leave the parties to themselves, in hope that other powers will pursue the same course."

Definitions

The Law of Beneficence: The discipline of dealing with what is good and evil, and with moral duty, and obligation.

Monroe Doctrine: An American doctrine of foreign policy in which the United States observed a strict policy of non-interference in the conflicts of other nations.

Writing Assignment

In 2 Chronicles 33, we are given the story of Manasseh, who was among the wicked kings in the ancient world. However, the Lord brought judgment to him, humbled him, and brought him to repentance. This is a testimony to God's grace and power to save. What should be our attitude toward wicked men who hold positions of civil power? Search the Scriptures and write at least 500 words on the attitude that a Christian Statesman ought to have concerning wicked rulers.

Recommendations for Further Study

John Calvin His Roots and Fruits, by C. Gregg Singer

The Great Christian Revolution, by Otto Scott

Aspects of Christian Social Ethics, by Carl F.H. Henry

The Collected Works of James M. Buchanan, by James M. Buchanan

American Political Writing During the Founding Era, by Charles S. Hyneman

Unit Seven–Lesson 5
The Attributes of
The Ruler of Nations

Introduction

God is the ruler of nations. He is the ultimate source of all authority and the final word on issues of law, ethics, and public policy. The righteousness of laws is determined by their conformity and constancy to His law-word. The nature and jurisdiction of earthly powers are limited according to the authority which He delegates. The inalienable rights of mankind are issued from Him. In essence the whole of creation is held together by Him.

This should give both the Christian and the non-Christian the utmost comfort with regard to matters of law, ethics, and public policy. This means, by implication, that all tyrannies will fail, all conspiracies will be exposed, every arbitrary law will be overturned, and every right and liberty of man is firmly established. We know the nature of God's rule by what the Bible tells us of His attributes. We know that God is a hidden and transcendent God who has revealed Himself and is intimately involved in our lives.

God is immutable. This means that He does not change. He is the same "yesterday, today, and forever."[48] In God there is no variableness or shadow of turning.[49] With regard to the rule of law, this is essential. It means that the principles that provide the framework for law, ethics, and public policy also do not change. It also means that God's plan for the nations has not changed and will not change. Our rights and liberties do not change but are secure in Him.

God is omniscient. This means God knows all things. His knowledge transcends both time and space. He sees from the beginning to the end of human history. This means that nothing in the world escapes His notice. There is no act of good that will go unrewarded and no crime will go unrecompensed. Even though there are those criminals who escape the justice of temporal authorities, the sentence of justice follows the criminal wherever he goes. Moreover, the omniscience of God means that the there is no uncertainty of the future. While temporal leaders may fail to plan for unexpected calamities, there is no disaster or unexpected calamity that God has not seen.

God is omnipotent. This means that God is powerful to do whatever He desires to do. "Our God is in the Heavens; He hath done whatsoever He hath pleased."[50] This means that none of His words shall fall short of accomplishment. None of His decrees will fail to come to pass. His promises are sure and reliable. Nothing can withstand or subvert His will for the nations. He will judge all of those that rebel against Him and will bless those who glorify Him. Nothing is beyond His reach and His government cannot fail.

God is holy. This means that all His judgments are perfect and good. There is no tyranny or oppression in the government of God. His law and judgments bring perfect justice. All of His laws are perfect in equity. His government gives freedom and redemption from all forms of slavery and bondage. God is intrinsically good all the time and in all ways. This means that injustice and corruption cannot occur in the government of God. Every thing that is done is good and for His glory.

Christians are citizens and ambassadors of the Kingdom of God, to the broken governments of this fallen world. In this lecture Paul Jehle will complete this three part series on the Law of Nations by talking about the change that took place in America from the time of the Civil War up to our modern time. He will describe how the United States lost its way when it ignored the Law of God. Finally, he will talk about ways in which America can repent and be reformed.

Lecture Outline

The Law of the Nations and American History

1. **The Importance of Delegated Authority**

    A. The goal of the Church to equip the saints to do the work of ministry

    B. The goal in the home is to train our children

2. **Constitutional Meaning of the Law of Nations**

    A. Internal equality standing before God

        i. No independence with a nation

        ii. No intermeddling with any nations

        iii. No intervention in any nation's conflict

3. **Interposition**

    A. Based on lawful intervention

    B. Just War Doctrine

4. **The Progressive Overthrow of the Law of Nations**

    A. 1867: Abraham Lincoln and the Civil War

        i. Started the trend of presidents taking jurisdictions that they did not have

    B. 1867: Andrew Johnson, the purchase of Alaska and the Possession of the Midway Island

    C. 1870: Ulysses Grant and the Santo Domingo & Samoan Islands

    D. 1881: Chester Arthur & a Confederation of Nations of North & South America

    E. 1889: Benjamin Harrison & the Bureau of American Republics

5. **President Grover Cleveland's Message and the Annexation of Hawaii: December 18, 1893**

6. **The Spanish-American War For the Treaty and Intervention: 1898; William McKinley**

7. Theodore Roosevelt's Corollary 1903-1914

    A. Acquiring of a ten mile Panama Canal Zone

8. Original Monroe Doctrine

    A. Limited to the Western Hemisphere

    B. Nations are sovereign; succeed or fail

    C. No intervention within another nation

    D. Interposition when U.S. is directly threatened through the re-conquering of one of the nations in this Hemisphere

    E. All war must be in self-defense

    F. No military expansion in peace time

9. Roosevelt Corollary Expansion

    A. No limitation, it is now global

    B. Good nations must police wicked nations

    C. Intervention for chronic "wrong-doing"

    D. Exceptional cases require intervention in order to prevent war or make sure the right side wins in a conflict

    E. A "strong arm" used to prevent war

10. Woodrow Wilson, the War to End All Wars; Peace Without Victory 1917-1918

11. An International Government: November 11, 1918 The Treaty of Versailles and the Covenant of the League of Nations

    A. The treaty did not restore justice, but acted in vengeance

12. Herbert Hoover and the Kellogg-Brand Pact Treaty for the Renunciation of War: 1929

    A. Peace at the price of justice

13. 1939: Neutrality Laws

14. 1945: Yalta and the Charter of the United States

A. The unequally yoked covenant with Russia (Stalin) sets the stage for the Cold War

15. United Nations

A. Wars- Korea and Vietnam to contain Communism, not defeat it

B. Financial and military aid to threatened nations in order to contain Communism

C. United States disarms in order to negotiate

D. United Nations disarms in order to negotiate with an avowed enemy bent on our destruction

16. Instances Developed in American Foreign Policy

A. Interdependence (Appeasement)

B. Intermeddling (Containment)

C. Interventionism (Disarmament)

7. War

A. "The most dreaded enemy of liberty"-James Madison, August 1793

18. The Importance of Having the Law of God in Our Hearts in Order to Win Nationally and Internationally

Questions

1. What should the intervention in other nations' conflicts be based on?

_____

_____

_____

2. What is the Constitutional meaning of the Law of Nations?

_____

_____

_____

3. What marks the beginning of the progressive overthrow of the Law of the Nations?

_____

_____

_____

4. Why is the purchase of Alaska problematic?

_____

_____

_____

5. Why is the message of President Grover Cleveland important?

_____

_____

_____

6. What are some issues facing Christian politicians when it comes to methods?

_____

_____

_____

7. What is interposition?

_____

_____

_____

8. How did President Roosevelt move away from the original Monroe Doctrine?

_____

_____

_____

9. What are some instances developed in American Public Policy?

_____

_____

_____

10. According to James Madison what is the most dreaded enemy of liberty and how would we implement the Law of the Nations once more?

_____

_____

_____

Selected Reading

In his *Institutes of the Christian Religion*, John Calvin address the issue of lawful resistance to tyranny:

> *"Herein is the goodness, power, and providence of God wondrously displayed. At one time he raises up manifest avengers from among his own servants, and gives them his command to punish accursed tyranny, and deliver his people from calamity when they are unjustly oppressed; at another time he employs, for this purpose, the fury of men who have*

other thoughts and other aims. Thus he rescued his people Israel from the tyranny of Pharaoh by Moses; from the violence of Chusa, king of Syria, by Othniel; and from other bondage by other kings or judges. Thus he tamed the pride of Tyre by the Egyptians; the insolence of the Egyptians by the Assyrians; the ferocity of the Assyrians by the Chaldeans; the confidence of Babylon by the Medes and Persians, Cyrus having previously subdued the Medes, while the ingratitude of the kings of Judah and Israel, and their impious contumacy after all his kindness, he subdued and punished, - at one time by the Assyrians, at another by the Babylonians. All these things, however, were not done in the same way. The former class of deliverers being brought forward by the lawful call of God to perform such deeds, when they took up arms against kings, did not at all violate that majesty with which kings are invested by divine appointment, but armed from heaven, they, by a greater power, curbed a less, just as kings may lawfully punish their own satraps. The latter class, though they were directed by the hand of God, as seemed to him good, and did his work without knowing it, had nought but evil in their thoughts.

But whatever may be thought of the acts of the men themselves, the Lord by their means equally executed his own work, when he broke the bloody scepters of insolent kings, and overthrew their intolerable dominations. Let princes hear and be afraid; but let us at the same time guard most carefully against spurning or violating the venerable and majestic authority of rulers, an authority which God has sanctioned by the surest edicts, although those invested with it should be most unworthy of it, and, as far as in them lies, pollute it by their iniquity. Although the Lord takes vengeance on unbridled domination, let us not therefore suppose that that vengeance is committed to us, to whom no command has been given but to obey and suffer. I speak only of private men. For when popular magistrates have been appointed to curb the tyranny of kings (as the Ephori, who were opposed to kings among the Spartans, or Tribunes of the people to consuls among the Romans, or Demarchs to the senate among the Athenians; and perhaps there is something similar to this in the power exercised in each kingdom by the three orders, when they hold their primary diets). So far am I from forbidding these officially to check the undue license of kings, that if they connive at kings when they tyrannize and insult over the humbler of the people, I affirm that their dissimulation is not free from nefarious perfidy, because they fraudulently betray the liberty of the people, while knowing that, by the ordinance of God, they are its appointed guardians."

Definitions

Intermeddling: The act of entering into the personal affairs of another.

Interventionism: An approach to foreign policy in which one nation intervenes in the conflicts of another nation in order to bring a desired outcome.

Writing Assignment

There are many theologians/statesmen who had a profound impact in shaping the western legal tradition. John Calvin, J. Gresham Machen, Robert L Dabney, Samuel Rutherford, John Knox, and Martin Luther are only a few of the men who provide testimonies of the importance of sound theology and its application to shaping matters of law, ethics, and public policy in their local communities and nations. Write a 500-word essay regarding the importance of the contributions of these men. Include a discussion concerning the importance that men in our own generation stand on the shoulders of these theologian statesmen and faithfully apply sound theology to every aspect of their lives and communities.

Recommendations for Further Study

The Legacy of John Calvin, by David W. Hall

The Works of John Knox, by John Knox

Constitutionalism and the Separation of Powers, by M.J.C. Vile

Constitutionalism: Ancient and Modern, by Charles Howard McIlwain

Magna Charta: A Commentary on the Great Charter of King John, with an Historical Introduction, by William Sharp McKechni

Answer Key

Unit One

Lesson 1

1. John Witherspoon trained a generation of leaders, vice-presidents, President James Madison, Supreme Court justices, 10 cabinet members, 12 governors, 21 senators, 31 representatives, numerous delegates to the Constitutional Convention; 1/6th of our founding fathers sat under his tutelage.

2. To learn about the importance of God's Law and to encourage a Hebrew style of education.

3. Greek education is individualistic, the child is believed to belong to the State; Hebrew education is relational, the child is a creation of God, part of the unfolding plan of God.

4. The Supreme Court upheld a law that prohibited women from practicing law.

5. God, the Creator of Heaven and Earth.

6. The purpose of law is to restrain evil. Law cannot make people righteous.

7. Yes, all men are equally religious.

8. Higher Criticism is the belief that men can judge what part of the Bible is reasonable and scientifically defensible. Lower criticism contracts the Bible to get the actual context and intent of the Word of God.

9. *Lex Rex* by Samuel Rutherford and *Aaron's Rod Blossoming* by George Gillespie.

10. Religion, Sovereignty, Faith, and Infallibility.

Lesson 2

1. Modern Christians have failed to influence the public square because they have become ashamed of the Gospel.

2. It means that you are self-conscious of how your actions line up with what you know to be true.

3. Because Scripture is the standard by which matters of law, ethics, and public policy are determined, and the aid of the Holy Spirit is essential as a guide to human reason.

4. All knowledge is deposited in the mind of Christ and to have the mind of Christ is to be renewed in our minds.

5. The Creator/Creature distinction demands that God's creatures have only one valid frame of reference, and that all men are obligated to glorify God whether they profess faith in Him or not.

6. The doctrine of the Sufficiency of Scripture means that the Scripture is sufficient to instruct us in every area of life and unto every good work.

7. Fideism is contradictory to a Christian epistemology because it holds that faith is not always reasonable; whereas, because God made the world the Christian view of epistemology holds that nothing can be known without reference to God.

8. Maxims and misconceptions of Scripture are dangerous and must be avoided because the Scripture is a book of authority and our conceptions of Scripture eventually become unbiblical human tradition.

9. The Commandment is interpreted as a relevant principle that a laborer is worthy of his hire and that the church should not fail to see to the financial support of the clergy.

10. The Law of God can be distinguished into three categories as follows: (1) laws pertaining to personal morality, (2) laws pertaining to social interaction, (3) laws pertaining to abrogated ceremony.

Lesson 3

1. We discover them in the book of Genesis.

2. The Doctrine of Atonement is the basis for the American Doctrine of Jurisprudence.

3. They are: Jurisdiction, Equality, Fault, Vow, Dominion, and Restitution.

4. The purpose of criminal law is to restore the criminal, to satisfy God's justice, and to make the victim whole.

5. Criminal Law, Tort Law, Evidence Law, Real and Personal Property Law, Contract Law, Constitutional Law, Civil Procedure.

6. That God as the Creator governs all creatures, actions, and things "by His most wise and holy providence according to His infallible foreknowledge and the free and immutable council of His own will" for His own glory.

7. Two witnesses were required.

8. The word *supine* means the failure to act or protest as a result of moral weakness. Under the legal doctrine of subpoena an individual has an obligation to appear before the court on the behalf of his neighbor to see justice be done.

9. Procedural law is concerning the procedure for which a case is brought and heard before the court. The Substantive Law is the standard by which a determination of justice is to be made.

10. The *Magna Charta* is an ancient source of constitutional rights, and it limits the Government's ability to lawfully impose in various areas of the civil realm.

Lesson 4

1. The debate is whether the Bible will be held out as the supreme authority or not.

2. Homosexuality, women fighting alongside men, unjustifiable warfare.

3. We should expect persecution and be faced with having to choose between our jobs and following Christ.

4. No, women should not hold civil office.

5. That it is more important that few people do well than many do wrong.

6. No. No matter what the outcome, we must always vote for a candidate who is biblically qualified.

7. The Church of Jesus Christ.

8. Paul's example found in Acts 17.

9. First, he points out the ignorance of their thinking, then he appeals to the doctrine of Creation and he ends with a call for repentance.

10. That we are witnesses for Jesus Christ.

Unit Two

Lesson 1

1. Yes, the priests, the scribes, and the elders, describe the three aspects of the Jewish Sanhedrin (the ruling council of Israel) so their questions are legitimate.

2. The fundamental questions of Government are: (1) by what authority? and (2) do you have jurisdiction?

3. The basic principle of the application of Scriptures is that God's law must be administered by the proper jurisdiction.

4. That Jesus has jurisdictional authority over everything including the self, the family, the church, and all nations.

5. God governs His creation through the Lordship of Jesus Christ.

6. Jesus governs all nations through the authority of God's Law.

7. That God is the Lord of the conscience and we are free from doctrines and commandments of men to serve God in righteousness and holiness before God all the days of our lives.

8. The invocation of judgment upon ones self if the oath made is broken.

9. The elements of the covenantal model are: transcendence, hierarchy, ethics, oaths, & sanctions, and successions.

10. None. All three are equally important.

Lesson 2

1. Aaron's rod is a symbol of authority.

2. Erastianism is the doctrine that the State is supreme over the Church in ecclesiastical matters.

3. The Church is the most important followed by the State and lastly the Family.

4. The Family, the Church, and the State are all equally under God and perform different duties given by God.

5. The rod of correction is the symbol for the family, the keys are the symbol for the Church, and the sword is the symbol for the State.

6. The issue addressed by George Gillespie is the Church-State relationship, and he refuted the errors of Erastianism.

7. The Reformers' view that the State is not over the Church or vice-versa.

8. The Church has the duty to protect itself from the State's usurpation.

9. We allow tyranny to rule in various spheres of government in which they were not intended to rule.

10. No. According to the 1st Amendment to the Constitution, Congress should make no laws respecting the establishment of religion.

Lesson 3

1. No. The State has only the right to address criminal matters.

2. No. Protective Services should cease to exist because it is not a valid function of the State.

3. The Church has the authority over the matters of the heart while the State has the authority over physical issues that are actually done.

4. It protects the people against unreasonable searches and seizures.

5. The methodology used with questioning the children.

6. Clarke-Stewart Study, 1989

7. It is a rule of evidence that disallows evidence illegally seized to be used in criminal prosecutions.

8. By having its activity described as a civil activity not a criminal one.

9. No. The 4th Amendment protects us from such invasion.

10. By rewarding "good answers," leading questions, suggestive techniques and peer-pressure.

Unit Three

Lesson 1

1. Ethical considerations are important because ethics is the discipline of dealing with what is good and bad and with moral duty and obligation.

2. We mean that every aspect of our lives should be in alignment with the sound doctrines that we confess from Scripture.

3. The Bible does not speak to all ethical questions and therefore the Christian must determine for himself what is good and evil in matters where there is neutrality.

4. We should look at the overarching principles, patterns, clear statements, and God's statues.

5. God has given us His written Word, which is exhaustively applicable to all faith and life.

6. The word *apologia* refers to a counselor's advocacy before a judge.

7. The first duty of every lawyer is to promote God's righteous order and to seek God's righteous justice for the client.

8. Loss of national identity, move towards global community, continuing departure from the Law of God, increased usurpation of family and church jurisdiction by the State, Gnosticism.

9. No. God's Word speaks with authority to every area of life, especially over matters of law, ethics, and public policy.

10. Pragmatism by its very nature supposes that man is more capable than God in making wise decisions with regard to practical matters. By its very nature it presupposes an ultimate benefit is to be gained from disobedience to God's Word.

Lesson 2

1. No. Christians should study and answer ethical questions from every area.

2. No, since according to the Bible the first duty of government is the protection of innocent life.

3. Public schools are wrong because the Bible does not give the government jurisdiction over education.

4. Some of the types of arguments are: hermeneutic, exegetical, and the broad, sweeping argument.

5. Killing is allowed in the Bible in (1) defense of self and others, (2) justifiable

warfare, and (3) performed by the State in capital punishment executions.

6. What is the first duty of government? The first duty of government is to protect innocent life.

7. Why was cremation viewed as pagan up to the 20th century? Cremation was viewed as pagan because of the Biblical patterns: burial, preservation (Ex, Jesus, Abraham, Moses), and the awaiting of the resurrection of the dead.

8. What is the difference between organ donation and organ harvesting? Organ donation takes place with the permission of the donors while organ harvesting takes place without the permission of the owner.

9. What is the difference between autopsy and fetal stem cell donation? In an autopsy the body is buried after the procedure is done while in a fetal stem cell donation the cell is completed obliterated.

10. Should we ever take the life of one to save another? No, God did not give us jurisdiction over life and death.

Lesson 3

1. In Common Law, citizens were responsible for their own self-defense and were responsible to come to the aid of others.

2. According to William Blackstone the purpose of a militia is to resist tyranny in the state, foreign invasions, and public uprisings.

3. Jeremy Bentham's program for restoring the peace was to send those who differed from the state to re-education camps.

4. The first full time police force appeared in Boston in 1836, but were only on duty during the day.

5. The gun show "loophole" is the ability of a private citizen to sell a gun without notifying the Government.

6. The gun registration laws in Canada have never once been used to solve a gun crime.

7. Campaign finance reform restricts the speech of individuals from speaking

about any candidate 30 days prior to an election.

8. The United Nations poses a threat by openly opposing gun ownership and then claiming jurisdiction over the citizens of member nations to cause them to appear before an international criminal court.

9. The Scripture teaches us to be persistent to petition the high powers and resilient in the face of temporary failure.

10. Citizens have the constitutional right to own standard military issue arms.

Lesson 4

1. A piece of eight was a silver coin minted in the Spanish empire after 1497. It was legal tender throughout the colonies and was the basis for the original United States Dollar.

2. A Bill of Credit is paper money, which supposedly has a redemption value for coined money.

3. The Eagle was coined by Congress according to the Gold Standard and was given a certain dollar value based on the valuation of silver against the gold standard. If the Eagle was a ruler, the value of the dollar was the thing measured by it.

4. It created an advantage by allowing Congress to allow foreign coins to be used as legal tender in the United States, which would allow various coins to find a place in the one world market.

5. The Congress of the Union States passed the Legal Tender Act of 1862 which allowed for paper money for the first time.

6. In these cases, the Supreme Court upheld an invented Congressional power to issue bills of credit, which is not an enumerated power of Congress in the Constitution.

7. The danger is that a bank generates more promises to pay debts on demand than the bank has the ability to pay when the public reaches a panic point and demands payment of the debt.

8. Because at that time a Federal Reserve Bank note was redeemable in gold or silver. With the seizure of gold the bank was relieved of its promise to pay the

debt represented by the Federal Reserve notes in gold or silver.

9. Because courts are reluctant and fearful to make sweeping changes, and the current unconstitutional monetary system cannot be undone with a single case. Congress enjoys the redistribution of wealth as a means to fund private interests.

10. It is important because it is essential to identify the problems in economic policy and avoid the risk involved with investments that are excessively entangled in the immoral and unconstitutional system.

Unit Four

Lesson 1

1. The first Monday after the second Wednesday in December following the appointment of the electors.

2. There are 51 presidential elections one for each state and the District of Columbia.

3. Because if fraud was detected in a single city or state, the electors may vote without completely delegitimizing the popular vote; there are in fact 51 elections to dilute cases of local fraud.

4. It provided that the election of the Senate would be determined by a popular vote and not by the state's legislatures as was the case prior to the ratification of the 17th amendment. As a result the states are not allowed to play a role in national legislation.

5. The Twelfth Amendment was passed by Congress which enabled electors to cast votes for a president and a vice president.

6. Because he surmised he would not win that election, but that if he were made Secretary of State under John Quincy Adams, he would be next in line for the presidency.

7. Because Rutherford B. Hays promised to remove troops from the South if elected to the presidency.

8. If one candidate received 269 and another candidate received 268, but

the remaining vote went to a third party, it would go to the House of Representatives, and the third party could win.

9. If there were a tie in the Electoral College; and if the houses of Congress failed to gather the necessary two-thirds majority needed to vote, there would be no president or vice president elect. In that case the Speaker of the House would become acting president until the presidency was determined.

10. Candidates would be able to focus on large cities and only represent certain segments of the population while ignoring less populated regions of the country. It would also break down the right of representation of all citizens in all areas of the nation.

Lesson 2

1. The Family, the State, and the Church.

2. John Knox

3. Headship involves the order God has established in every sphere of government in which the head is the covenant representative of those over whom he has authority.

4. 1 Corinthians 11:3 establishes the hierarchical structure of the world that the head of every man is Christ and the head of the woman is the man.

5. They must be men, wise and understanding, known among the community as having good character, and must have the fear of God.

6. Because at Creation we learn that God created the woman to be a perfect help to the man and was not to rule over him or be his superior. Therefore, the idea of a female magistrate is against nature itself.

7. The Scripture tells us that a woman is to be a keeper at home, to serve the family economy, her husband, and is to be the mother of children.

8. It is lamented in Scripture and it is described as a type of judgment.

9. Deborah is a poor example since there is no evidence that she was a civil magistrate, but rather she was a prophetess who advised civil magistrates.

Instead Barack carried out that practical role of a judge.

10. Christians will not be able to stand against the threats of feminism and egalitarianism if we are unable or unwilling to strictly apply the Word of God to these issues. Moreover, if we fail to apply the Word of God in this area of life concerning women, we lose the ability to forbid the leadership of women in the Church and even over their husbands in the sphere of the family.

Unit Five

Lesson 1

1. Sovereignty and accountability.

2. The rights to life, liberty, and the pursuit of happiness.

3. They are limited to implementing policies that have been enacted by the Legislature and signed into law.

4. The Supreme Court has ruled that they have a property interest in their jobs and it is very difficult to remove them from their positions even when they refuse to obey direct orders.

5. Only Congress may constitutionally regulate trade with foreign nations. NAFTA allows for foreign lawmakers to vote on trade regulation in the United States. Nor are rules created by NAFTA required to obtain a two/thirds majority in the U.S. Senate for ratification.

6. The President could declare abortion unconstitutional and would hire U.S. Attorneys who would prosecute abortionists for their assault on the life and liberty of an unborn child. He could also impound federal funding for abortion by declaring it an allocation for an unconstitutional purpose.

7. Because the Christian agenda must be God's agenda, and both parties hold to positions which are unabashedly unbiblical.

8. Because the President and Congress allow for a private banking group to set monetary policy and print currency in the United States.

9. It is difficult for a third party to successfully run for the presidency because the

two major parties have instituted restrictions on the state level which make it very hard to even get on the ballot nationwide.

10. Incrementalism is based on a system in which compromise is made a prerequisite for its operation and for its success. Incrementalism often falls short because with every step forward it requires two steps in the wrong direction.

Unit Six

Lesson 1

1. Jurisprudence is the study of the nature, content, and purpose of law.

2. That the Word of God is the only infallible source of truth and that God is the Sovereign Lord of all things.

3. The law that is actually and specifically enacted by proper authority for the government of society; the law of the State.

4. Law is exclusively the product of public consciousness and evolution.

5. The theory that the only valid law is the one that can be empirically verified.

6. No, distinctions between bad law and good law have to be made according to moral criteria.

7. The belief that law is the will of a Sovereign power and can be verified in an objective way, if applied to God's government.

8. Human reasoning and the false notion that the natural world is a source of law.

9. Classical, medieval, and modern.

10. Special revelation is God's revelation through His Word and general revelation is God's revelation through the natural world that He created.

11. The prideful assumption that man can know good and evil apart from God's word.

12. No, it is in opposition to Scriptures.

Lesson 2

1. George Washington's first official act was to offer supplication to Almighty God.

2. The First Amendment to the United States Constitution only places a limitation on the Federal Congress.

3. Congress called on the President to declare a day of prayer and fasting.

4. Over 400,000, without a trial or presentation of evidence.

5. Because he upheld his oath of office and followed the example of America's founders in acknowledging the sovereignty of God.

6. It proposed that the states should abandon the acknowledgement of God in the civil realm, and instead be established on the reason of man.

7. Because when the sovereignty of God is denied the tyrannous sovereignty of man is imposed.

8. The advent of gay rights and abortion are products of a judiciary that has turned away from God.

9. Immorality will reign and men will do every thing that seems right in their own eyes.

10. Because the Constitution declares that the Constitution, the laws of Congress, and duly ratified treaties shall be the supreme law of the land

Lesson 3

1. The keys are symbolic of the authority and the power of the government of the church to practice church discipline.

2. The word *appoint* in the Greek means to elect by a show of hands.

3. The standard by which the local church is to be governed is the entire written Word of God.

4. In the Scriptures, elders and bishops are interchangeable. Instead, the term elder signifies the dignity of the office, and the term bishop signifies the function of the office.

5. A presbytery is a term used to describe a plurality of elders officially meeting together to oversee the life of the church.

6. Through the preaching of the Gospel and the writing of confessions of faith.

7. That God requires man to worship him in the manner that he has instructed man to worship him without the presence of human innovation.

8. The Scripture requires a creditable profession of faith as a prerequisite for local church membership.

9. According to Matthew 18, the entire congregation is involved in counseling and church discipline to some degree. The involvement of the elders of the church and the exclusion from membership in the church is an advanced stage of the process of church discipline.

10. The purpose of civil courts is to execute justice against the wicked works of evildoers and to restore individuals who have been victimized by them.

Unit Seven

Lesson 1

1. The Reformed position is that the Word of God must be the foundation for every area of life.

2. The three tiers of God's Law are the two greatest commandments found in Matthew 22:37-40, the Ten Commandments, and the case laws.

3. The moral Law of God always existed, based on the holy character of God, unchangeable.

4. Some of the law principles found in Genesis are: jurisdiction of all authority, equality of all men, the establishment of covenants, criminal justice, judicial authority, principles of war, and arms.

5. Equality of all men means that we are all equally subject to the same laws.

6. Some of the commandments are: worship God not the snake, do not commit idolatry, keep the Sabbath, honor our fathers, do not lie, do not steal, do not covet.

7. The case laws illustrate how the two greatest commandments found in Matthew 22:37-40 and the Ten Commandments are applied in different cases.

8. Some of the areas are: criminal law, tort law, evidence law, real and personal property law, and contract law.

9. That Christ did away with the law, that there is tension between law and grace, and that to believe in the relevance of the law is to believe that the law saves us.

10. The purpose and direction of the law is the restitution of God's order.

Lesson 2

1. This case encompasses the evolutionary thinking that governs our nation.

2. By what standard?

3. Positive Law is the belief that men can create law out of nothing that becomes truth by majority action.

4. To be "epistemologically self-conscious" is to be aware of your worldview and its implications on life. It is to know how you get from A to Z.

5. Presupposition is an elementary assumption. A basic commitment. A foundational perspective in which experiences and facts are interpreted.

6. Idolatrous false worship, child sacrifice, moral perversion, and effeminacy and abdication by men.

7. *A Model of Christian Charity*.

8. According to Blackstone, law is "a rule of action dictated by a superior being."

9. According to Van Til, the Bible is a "source book "for all truth.

10. The First Amendment prevented the federal government from usurping state rights by discriminating between Christian denominations and from restricting the right of the states to establish state churches.

Lesson 3

1. The Christian should place his loyalty in the Kingdom of Heaven.

2. Satan's government is structured from the top down.

3. He begins to structure His government in the heart of man.

4. They originate from groups of families.

5. It will have the elements of sanctity, sanctions, and redemption.

6. The Ten Commandments.

7. God is the source of American Law.

8. The violation of the personal covenant with God produces the greatest consequences.

9. The Marriage Covenant.

10. Hugo Grotius.

Lesson 4

1. That an individual should be under the authority of government.

2. The Creator God who rules the nations.

3. The two nations must be equally yoked.

4. He did not mean that it was written by the people, but rather that it was binding on the people.

5. No because God has not given jurisdiction to America to police the internal affairs of other nations.

6. They observed a policy of non-intervention.

7. The Monroe Doctrine was a position in foreign policy that the United States would not intermeddle in the affairs of other nations.

8. Because the president does not have the power to declare war.

9. The Congress.

10. That the United States did nothing to help Texas win independence.

Lesson 5

1. It should be based on the law of God and not pragmatism.

2. The Law of Nations is based on an internal equality standing before God, with some characteristics being: no independence with a nation, no intermeddling with any nations, and no intervention in any nation's conflict.

3. The presidency of Abraham Lincoln and the Civil War marks the beginning of the trend of presidents taking jurisdictions they did not have.

4. Because it is the first territory obtained promising citizenship without incorporation into State-wood, a trend toward imperialism.

5. He recognizes the Law of the Nations and takes a step back from the trend of presidents taking jurisdictions that are not theirs: Hawaiian example.

6. They have to choose from "Christianizing" pagan methods to get immediate goals or live for multigenerational vision according to God's Word.

7. Interposition is a theory for resistance to tyranny in witch a lower magistrate with authority may resist the tyranny of a higher magistrate.

8. By asserting some principles such as: good nations must police wicked nations, intervention for chronic wrong-doing, exceptional cases require intervention in order to prevent war or make sure the right side wins in a conflict, a "strong-arm" used to prevent war.

9. Interdependence, intermeddling, and interventionism.

10. According to Madison, war is the enemy of liberty; having God's Law in our hearts would help us implement the Law of the Nations once more.

End Notes

Unit One

Lesson 1

1. Rousas J. Rushdoony, *This Independent Republic*, (Thornburg Press; Fairfax Virginia, 1978) p. 21

2. Matthew 7: 17-20, 24-29

3. James Madison, *The Records of the Federal Convention of 1787*, Editor, Max Farrand, (Yale University Press; New Haven, Ct.: 1966) vol. 1, pp. 451-452

Lesson 2

4. Joshua 2:12

Lesson 3

5. R.J. Rushdoony, *Studies in Early Genesis*, Audio, no. 1 *The Closed Universe of Evolution*

6. Declaration of Independence, Preamble

Lesson 4

7. F.F. Bruce, *The Canon of Scripture*, (InterVarsity Press; Downers Grove, IL: 1988) p. 17

8. Westminster Confession of Faith, Ch. 1, Sec. 2

9. Matthew 5:19-20

10. Matthew 23

11. Luke 12:1

12. Henry Van Til, *The Calvinistic Concept of Culture*, (Baker Academic; Grand Rapids, MI: 2001) p. 200

13. Leonard Verduin, *The Reformers and their Stepchildren*, (The Baptist Standard Bearer; Paris AK: 1964) p. 23

Unit Two

Lesson 1

14. Matthew 28:18

15. Acts 2:36

16. Samuel Adams, "The Divine Source of Liberty," *The Patriot's Handbook*, ed. George Grant, (Elkton, MD: Highland Books, 1996), p. 86

17. Clarence Manion, *The Key to Peace*, (Chicago, IL; Heritage Foundation: 1951) p. 91, cited from, R.J. Rushdoony, *This Independent Republic*, (Fairfax, VA; Thoburn Press: 1978)

Lesson 2

18. Greg L. Bahnsen, *By This Standard* (AV Press; Powder Springs, GA, 2008) p. 204

19. Robert Joseph Renaud & Lael Daniel Weinberger, *Spheres of Sovereignty: Church Autonomy Doctrine and the Theological Heritage of the Separation of Church and State*, 35 N. Ky. L. Rev. (2008) p. 67

20. George Gillespie, *Aaron's Rod Blossoming*, (Sprinkle Publications; Harrisonburg, VA: 2002) pp. 117, 121

21. Charles F. James, *Documentary History of the Struggle for Religious Liberty in Virginia*, (Sprinkle Publications; Harrisonburg, VA: 2007) supra, at 73

22. John Eidsmoe, *Christianity and the Constitution*, (Baker Books; Grand Rapids, MI) pp. 110-111

Lesson 3

23. John Calvin, *Commentary on the Book of Genesis, Vol. I*, p. 224

24. B.M. Palmer, *The Family*, (Harrisonburg, VA; Sprinkle Publications 1991) p. 9

25. Cotton Mather, *A Family Well-Ordered*, (Soli Deo Gloria Publications 2001) p. 1

26. Kollontai, *Communism and the Family*, p. 17

27. Paul Johnson, *Modern Times*, (New York: NY; Harper Perennial, 2001) p. 581

Unit Three

Lesson 1

28. James McClellan, *Liberty, Order, and Justice*, (Liberty Fund, Indianapolis, IN, 2000) p. 3

29. Cotton Mather, *Bonifacius*, (Kessinger Publishing; Whitefish, MT, 2003) p. 40, 41

Lesson 2

--

Lesson 3

30. John Calvin, *The Institutes of the Christian Religion*, Bk. 4, Ch. 20, Sec. 1, trans. Henry Beveridge, (Grand Rapids, MI; WM. B. Eerdman's Publishing Co., 1953) p. 651

Lesson 4

31. Proverbs 11:1

Unit Four

Lesson 1

32. John Jackson Kilpatrick, *The Sovereign States*, (H. Regnery Co: Chicago Il, 1957) p. 1

33. James McClellan, *Liberty, Order, and Justice*. p. 16

Lesson 2

34. Isaiah 3:11-13

Unit Five

Lesson 1

35. United States Constitution Article 2, Section 1

Unit Six

Lesson 1

36. Alexander Hamilton, Federalist Papers #78

37. Alexander Hamilton, James Madison, John Jay, *The Federalist Papers*, no. 78, (New American Library; New York, NY, 2000) p. 433

38. R.L. Dabney, *The Morality of the Legal Profession*, Discussions Vol. III, Sprinkle publications; Harrisonburg Va.; 1996) p. 6

Lesson 2

39. Alexander Hamilton, *The Federalist Papers*, #78

Lesson 3

40. Acts 15

41. Acts 21:18-23

42. 1 Corinthians 6:1-7

43. Acts 18:15

Unit Seven

Lesson 1

--

Lesson 2

--

Lesson 3

44. John 18:36
45. John 19: 15
46. Luke 19:13

Lesson 4

47. Psalm 9:4-5, Amos 1:3

Lesson 5

48. Malachi 3:6
49. James 1:17
50. Psalm 115:3